Bill
& Tonya
Macdonald

To my great-nephew Nicholas
Knatchbull who will I hope inherit
his parents', grandparents' and
great-grandparents' love of the
country, and be able to enjoy in his
generation his ancestors' patronage
of Capability Brown as architect and
landscape gardener.

Other books by David Hicks

David Hicks on Decoration (1966)
David Hicks on Living – with Taste (1968)
David Hicks on Bathrooms (1968)
David Hicks on Decoration – with Fabrics (1971)
David Hicks on Decoration – 5 (1972)
The David Hicks Book of Flower Arranging (1976)
David Hicks Living with Design (1979)

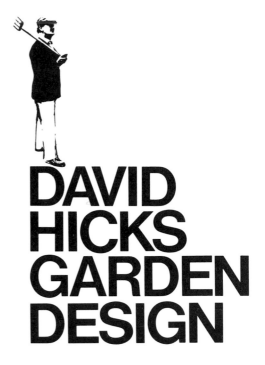

DAVID HICKS GARDEN DESIGN

Photographs and drawings by
David Hicks

Designed by
Nicholas Jenkins

Consultant Editor
Andrew Wheatcroft

Routledge & Kegan Paul
London, Boston and Henley

First published in 1982
by Routledge & Kegan Paul Ltd
39 Store Street, London WC1E 7DD
9 Park Street
Boston, Mass. 12108
and Broadway House
Newtown Road, Henley-on-Thames
Oxon RG9 1EN
Set in Monophoto Univers 685
and printed in Great Britain by
Westerham Press Ltd, Westerham,
Kent

ISBN 0 7100 9228 8
ISBN 0 7100 9239 3 Pbk

[handwritten notes:]

silver leaf
eriginom
Pale pink impatiens

get 4" Dickie
lust NOW
use ivy screen
behind it or?
(with thin yew
under)
flanked
by roses

Sea gull & other ramblers

on

Home-
made,
rustic.
Elm?

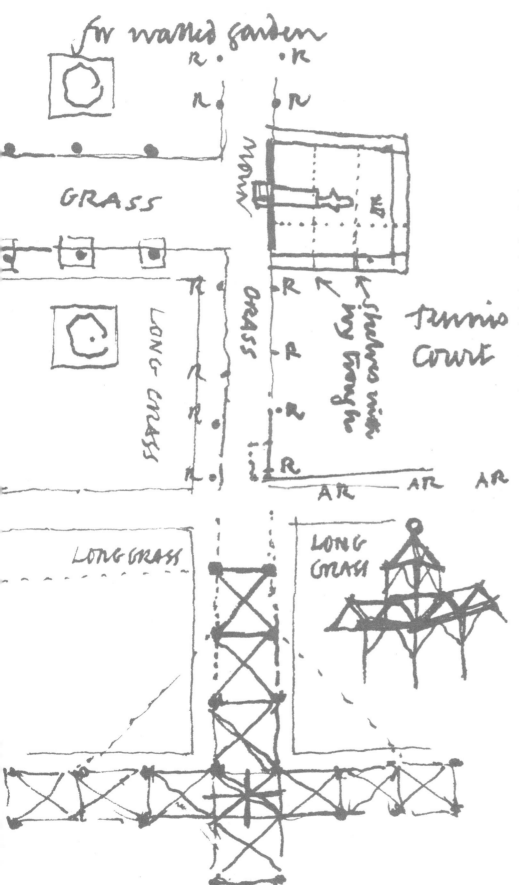

Acknowledgments

I am most grateful to:

The National Trust
The Trustees of the Grimsthorpe and
    Drummond Castle Estate
The Wardens of Gunston Hall
The Board of Trustees of Mount
    Vernon
The Trustees of Dumbarton Oaks
The Countess Beauchamp
The Comte de Brissac
Mr Roderick Cameron
The Carvallo family at the Château
    de Villandry
The Duke and Duchess of
    Devonshire
Mr Francis Egerton
Mr and Mrs Basil Feilding
Mr Nicolas Haslam
The Lord Hesketh
The Viscount De L'Isle
Mrs Claude Lancaster
Mr Christopher Lloyd
Mrs James Lees-Milne
The Duchesse de Mouchy
The Countess Munster
Mr Nigel Nicolson
The Duke and Duchess of Rutland
The Duchesse de Sabrans
The Lord Sackville
The Marchioness of Salisbury
Mrs Reginald Sheffield
Mr Reresby Sitwell
Lady Law-Smith
Lady Caroline Somerset
Mr John Stephanidis
Lady Anne Tree
Madame Pierre Vulliod
The Baronne Geoffroi de Waldener

and many other owners who
allowed me to photograph their
wonderful gardens.

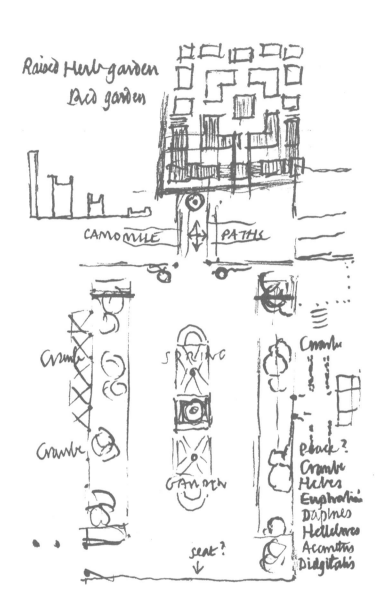

Raised Herb garden
Bed garden

CAMOMILE   PATHS

Crambe

Crambe

S PRING

GARDEN

Crambe

Pback?
Crambe
Helres
Euphorbia
Daphnes
Hellebores
Acanthus
Digitalis

seat?
↓

Contents

□ I have photographed my favourite gardens, mostly in England and France, including my own, barely a year old, to illustrate my passionate interest in garden design.

□ I have a very defined attitude towards style in gardens and few people would want to be as severe in their approach as I am. My aim is to explain my own sense of style and design.

□ A garden that pleases me is a garden that has style. In order to evoke style in a garden, it must be designed with deliberation. In setting out to plant an entirely new garden, or to modify or embellish an existing one, look at gardens open to the public and photographs and plans of gardens. By selecting those elements which you like you will evolve your own particular style. Never slavishly copy somebody else's look or design. Your soil, situation, house, existing boundary walls or aspect may not accommodate somebody else's scheme. It is always foolish simply to imitate, without considering the effect it will create in your own circumstances. I freely admit that the best of ideas in my own garden are adapted from those of other people whose taste I admire. But I have never attempted exactly to reproduce somebody else's solution, their way of planting, or mixing plants, or of using trees and ornaments.

□ Have the courage of your own ideas, and remember that rules can be broken. There are some practical horticultural constraints which do have to be accepted, but, being a great believer in experiment, if something is not doing well, in a particular place, I move it. If it is not happy it is never likely to achieve the effect you want, so try it somewhere else. It is useful to have your soil analysed, as this determines what you can grow successfully.

□ I have been interested in gardens from my youth. My first memory of a garden is when I was about six. It was very small and probably excruciatingly ugly, depending, as I remember, almost entirely on seeds bought at Woolworths. Not that I despise annuals; indeed to this day I still buy them from ordinary shops as well as from specialist firms and produce excellent results to augment my permanent planting.

□When I was sixteen, my mother and I moved to a Suffolk cottage, which had just three old apple trees in a paddock, and I helped to design what became quite a successful garden. The first thing we did was to drive a long, straight gravel path off-centre down the length of the garden; and then at right angles, another one on a lower level, reached by three wide brick steps. On the right-hand side of this, and parallel to it, we built an 'aerated' brick wall, only four feet high because of cost, with alternate bricks left out. At the end of this walk we built a five foot high square brick column, with a late eighteenth-century cast iron urn on it, that I bought for 50p in a Coggeshall builder's yard. Not yet knowing enough about plants, it had on either side of it what I can only describe as ordinary herbaceous borders. But it had a modicum of style, because of the design.

□ The next garden I tackled, ten years later, consisted of two very small areas on either side of an eighteenth-century fishing pavilion that I rented. I started by flanking the building with lines of hornbeam trees and hedges, the trees being planted six foot and the hedges a foot high. Fortunately the pavilion was on a formal canal, and the garden was very damp and the trees grew with amazing alacrity. Behind these flanking green architectural walls, I formed two small green rooms; one had a lawn and a second green wall while the other was filled with a large bed of old roses. Between these areas beside the road I put a line of limes.

□ As an interior designer, I have always been attracted to gardens which have a great sense of containment, not dissimilar to rooms — sheltered areas, with apertures leading excitingly on to other areas forming ideal backgrounds for the different planting in each section. Naturally this kind of garden approach has appealed to me from very early on because it is so similar to my interior designing work. I have been fascinated by all gardens which have this sense of open-air rooms; seats, urns, specimen trees — and flower beds — are the equivalent of furniture, sculpture, pictures and carpets.

□ The whole concept of growing things which you have sown yourself, pricked out, transplanted, watered, and fed, gives enormous satisfaction. Though as a designer, not merely content producing flowers and foliage nurtured from seeds onwards, I like to control the scale, the variety of texture and colour, the placing of different forms and shapes into a designed entity. That is not to say that I despise or reject in any way natural, attractive, unsophisticated aspects of nature. Some of the most pleasing visual memories are of a fine old tree on the edge of natural forest, or of extraordinary contorted Arthur Rackham-like roots of beech trees, half washed out of their chalky bed by the elements. But in the garden or roof garden, which relates immediately to a house or an apartment, I feel the need for controlled, designed order. I adore formal lines of trees for measured, formal garden architecture.

□ When I talk of lines of trees I do not necessarily mean a great avenue, I refer to an ordinary town garden, or small country one, perhaps fifteen feet by forty. The lines of trees down the outer longer perimeter, and a feature, whether it be a piece of modern sculpture, or an arbour at the end with regularly devised beds, can give great style and atmosphere. Because of the design it can be rewarding for all twelve months of the year. On the other hand, I know many people who have opted for the alternative attitude — an overgrown, semi-wild, romantic garden.

□ I dare say the kind of garden which you choose to construct around where you live reflects in a penetrating way your character. My own taste is for a formal structure near the house not obscuring the natural planting of previous generations just beyond.

□ This book is not botanical and was purposely illustrated in black and white (even the colour pages are 'all green' gardens) to demonstrate *garden design* and the importance of layout and planning, an importance, to my mind, overriding the actual selection of plants or trees in making a really satisfying garden.

David Hicks

☐ When I was seventeen, I saw Versailles for the first time, but at that time knew Villandry only from photographs. Impressive though Versailles is in every way, it is Villandry which has been the greater influence and inspiration. Each visit to Villandry is perhaps more exciting than the last. For me it is one of the seven wonders of the world, with its enveloping sense of green architecture, the broad expanse of the *Clos d'Eau*, the pollarded limes, and the clipped hornbeam walls. But there is also, as a complete contrast, the vegetable and flower garden — beautifully reconstructed early in this century. Villandry, in the rolling landscape of Touraine, above all other great gardens, has ideas for large, medium and small gardens. It provides inspiration

1

2

1. These clipped hornbeams planted in 1947 by John Fowler were the first architectural trees I saw and had a great influence on my attitude to garden design.
2/3/4. Villandry, as replanted at the turn of the century, has been enormously influential.

5

for those with ambitious, moderate or miniature schemes in mind. What pleases me most is the true and totally disciplined sense of tonal gardening – green on green on green.

☐ When I was nineteen I was fortunate enough to meet Vita Sackville-West at Sissinghurst, and later on got to know John Fowler and his wonderful hornbeam architecture at The Hunting Lodge, near Odiham. These two English gardens have had the greatest influence on my taste in garden design. And today, Mrs Claude Lancaster, Lady Caroline Somerset, Mr Roderick Cameron and Lady Law-Smith are all gardeners whom I admire tremendously, while Mr Francis Egerton must have the best small city garden in the world.

3

4

5. Chiswick House has a magical garden full of superb statuary which I saw first as a very young man.
6. French gardens with their geometric approach have always intrigued me – the Jardin du Paradis at the Duc de Sabran's chateau d'Ansouis sums this up.

☐ Mrs Lancaster lives in a cottage in the stable yard of her last home, Haseley Court. She is still a creative working gardener, out at the earliest hours tending the lovely garden reminiscent of her youth in Virginia. I think her great talent is a sure knowledge of plants and the unexpected way in which she uses them. David and Caroline Somerset made the garden at their house in Badminton with the help of Russell Page. The basic elements were a fine old yew hedge and some good walls. It is to my mind one of the best examples of post-war planting and design in England. Rory Cameron achieved, for me, total perfection in his garden at Saint-Jean, Cap Ferrat, with his sure knowledge of texture, contrast and scale. Joan Law-Smith, who does

1

beautiful water colours of flowers, has accomplished a wonderfully serene, cool, green and white garden in Victoria, Australia.

☐ All these influences have helped me to form my own personal style in gardening, which is surely one of the great pleasures in life.

1/2. Totally opposite influences on my approach to gardens are Villandry and Haseley.

2

Influences

The garden at Villandry.

1. Pollarded limes give unique character all through the year.
2. Gunston Hall, near Washington DC, has great magic. This stylish green garden was originally planted in 1760.

1. The great canal at Erddig, where the National Trust
has replanted the original garden layout with great care.
2. I saw Sissinghurst first in 1949 and it had a decisive
influence on me.

1

The pleached lime walk at Sissinghurst in the spring.

☐ The temptation to plant the largest possible
specimens is very great and I have on several occasions
in my life planted trees over 6 feet tall in architectural
lines in order to get a quick effect. The danger, of
course, with trees of this size is that they do need
enormous care during the first years. It must be
remembered that the shock of transplanting at that
stage is considerable; and so they will not go forward
very much for the first two or three years in the ground.
In fact I find that when large trees are put in, for the first
summer, they do not even form their leaves properly. It
is absolutely essential to prepare a really thorough
foundation for new trees — fertiliser and ground bark
mixed in the soil when planting, keeping the ground
around the base clear, and applying mulch or ground
bark to the bare earth around the newly-planted tree.
Above all, keep them well watered. When considering
specimen trees dotted around, it must be remembered
that even the most efficient of us can forget one
specimen tree during a dry summer. There is so much to
do during that vital, exciting June/July period, when
everything needs attention, that these outlying trees
may be forgotten. Buy from specialist tree nurseries and

Immediately young trees are planted in architectural
lines they give a sense of design to a garden. The
necessary posts and wires on which to support and
train them add weight to the effect of the new planting.

remember to stake them really well. Tread them in very firmly and use guards against rabbits and hares.

☐ For people who are incredibly impatient for results it is possible to build wooden fences or brick walls to form immediate architectural divisions between different parts of gardens. But, generally speaking, it must be said that, although patience is required in every aspect of garden planning, yew is remarkably quicker than many people think and, although most nurserymen will warn one against box edging on account of its slowness and the amount of work it takes, it really does pay dividends remarkably quickly and you just have to be patient.

☐ When you first take over an established garden, you should live with it for a year and see what the previous owners had in it, how well things do, what the colours of the various roses and herbaceous plants are, and label things during that first spring, summer and autumn, so that you will know whether they should be thrown away, kept where they are, or moved to a position where their colour is going to be more telling. Most plants do not mind being moved providing you move them at the right time of year — when they are dormant.

All successful modern gardens are essentially personal; it is true of great gardens and small gardens, gardens of town or country, and it is this sense of individual choice and determination which makes them interesting to look at. I personally look at all sorts of gardens with the same visual judgment which I use when visiting an art gallery, a museum or an historic house. I have a limited capacity for visual appreciation, and it is for this reason that I have always used a *selective eye*. When I am going round an exhibition of pictures, I am looking at paintings from the point of view – 'Do I really like it enough to want it for myself?' It is a very good way of *editing* what you are looking at, because you cannot take everything in when looking at a vast collection. So I dart from one thing to another, using my sense of discrimination to select those things which I particularly want to remember. So, when looking at a garden, discard those elements which are of no interest to you: concentrate your senses and your analysis on those things which appeal. Test them – do you like them enough to want to adapt or modify them for your garden? If not, forget them. If they pass the test, assess them in detail – see how they work, and how they could be made to work for you. Gardens are infinitely complex, and, without some means of editing out distracting ideas, can be seen only as a vague collection of effects, rather than a set of ideas applied and followed through. All good gardens have some principle of organisation, even the wildest and most unkempt. Look behind the superficial elements to what lies beneath.

The gardens I prefer are those that have planting and layout which concentrate on visual effect rather than a collection of numerous botanical specimens. I do not despise – indeed I admire – those gardeners whose sole aim is the variety and size of their collection of rare and unusual plants. But these are not the gardens I enjoy most, and it is not the kind of garden that I plant for myself. There is, of course, the element of the collector in all serious gardeners. In some it becomes focused on a single area or species. I know of gardeners who have amassed collections of lilies, or old roses, or fritillaries, or alpines, or ericas. While I would never consider myself a collector to this degree of intensity, I do confess to an abiding passion for old roses. In a sense I do collect them. But I very often lose their labels, and my collection is certainly not exhaustive. There are some old roses which I actually do not like, and in my collection I mix modern and hybrid tea roses, because almost every true old rose has a carmine or shocking pink colour – strong or muted. Because of this recurrent blue-red blue-pink theme in old roses, I like to mix modern hybrids because they introduce the corals and the orange colours, which to me make the old pinks and cerises so much more exciting.

When I am picking and arranging old roses, I always like to mix some of the new colours not obtainable in the old varieties. So, in front of me as I write, I have Paul

1

2

Neyron, Mme Isaac Pereire, Constance Spry, and the dark-coloured and highly-scented Etoile de Hollande, and strong vermilion red Super Star which is ideally suited to the rich venetian red walls of my London apartment. Nor would I be without the pleasure of a snippet of that winter jasmine — which normally flowers in my greenhouse in February, and which sometimes produces a late second flowering in July. I mix it with two sprigs of Dutch honeysuckle, and *Lilium regale*, with its white trumpets, also blooming in July; and on the other side of the vase I have Belle de Crécy, with a Normanby Park geranium and two Albertine roses for scent.

☐ Few roses rival the strong but delicate, delicious scent of Albertine. She is blowzy, spiky and difficult to manage; but she does produce the most spectacular results on a wall, and in a room. I grow her for two identically rewarding reasons: to look great outside, and to infuse a room with her presence, and she does bloom for about four weeks.

☐ Old-fashioned roses must be given a very minor part in the general structure of the garden, for their blooming time, with a few notable exceptions, is so terribly short — wonderful, magic moments though they are. They are, however, like love affairs — short and very sweet. Equally sadly, their brevity in the garden is matched by their short life as cut flowers indoors. Not, of course that one discounts many of them for their foliage throughout the leafed season — which can be remarkably varied,

from the greyish-green of the Alba roses, the deeply veined bright green leaves of the *rugosa*, and the deep red overlaid with a greyish/blue bloom of the *rubrifolia*. Perhaps even more rewarding is the bright acid green of the climber Wedding Day. It is of some significance in the structure of the garden that they can form quite massive plants when fully developed.

☐ The charm and the sense of surprise that can be achieved by creating outdoor rooms in gardens is to my mind one of the most exciting elements of gardens. Surprise, contrast, not seeing everything at once, are the elements which give such pleasure.

☐ Of course walled gardens, however small, have that same element of contained space and there is a very real practical benefit from this kind of compartmentalisation in that it does afford considerable protection against frost and it creates warm areas when the sun is about; it also protects some delicate plants from the wind, that arch-enemy of some of our best plants.

☐ The sense of far-off trees peeping over the top of these enclosed areas is exciting and gives a dimension of distance, which is important. Scale, of course, must be one of the most significant qualities to consider when laying out the design of your garden or adapting an existing framework to your own ideas. Sir George Sitwell wrote a complete book on the contemplation of garden design and he turned Renishaw into one of the most successful gardens in England.

3

1. Stones, grass, fruit and flowers, combine delightfully in a French garden.
2. Mr David Somerset adapted this pedimented doorway in a wall for his garden from a detail at Badminton House. Pierced wooden gates at the far end of the vista lead the eye through.
3. At Kew Palace, outside London, a disciplined formal garden has been planted in the late seventeenth-century manner.

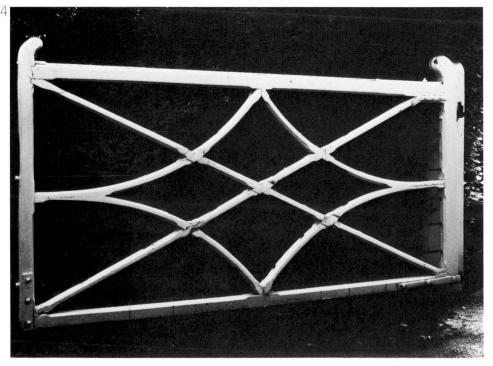

1

2

4

1. These gates, inspired by early eighteenth-century garden boundary design, are painted a strange blue-green, which looks superb under the dappled shade of an *allée* through a handsome stand of beech trees.
2. Good looking Edwardian gate and fencing in Nottinghamshire.
3. A Victorian gate in Yorkshire.
4. A late nineteenth-century painted gate in Kent.
5. Stylish solution for a gateway leading to a large wood.

3

5

☐ The earliest gardens were contained for very practical reasons — privacy, exclusion of vermin, and to limit the area of cultivated ground. But they always had apertures — one was always able to look out and beyond to the forest, park, or arable fields often through *clairvoyées* — wide openings with metal railings. Walls were built for protection of the plants on them and the plants within the walled area, as well as for keeping out intruders. Very early on hedges of yew and holly were used to provide a sense of containment.

☐ Every detail of the garden plan and its perimeter must be decisive. The design you use for your entrance gate and the colour of the drive, the colour and texture of brick and mortar you use for a wall, the colour of the cement, which must be related to the type of brick, and the effect you intend, the sort of fence or hedge — all these elements are vitally important. In a sense, the boundaries and divisions are like the binding of a book — the handsome externals which announce a well-presented interior.

1. This gate and railings join the as-yet-unrestored stable block to the main house at Tytherope Park.
2. Fine beech hedge surmounting an old brick wall.
3. A delightful pierced gate leading into a walled garden: white posts and chain are practical and decorative.

3

1. Yew and beech hedges at Sissinghurst. Note the slender elegant span of the yew hedge.

2. In a cottage garden: the beech hedge has a romantic arch of honeysuckle over the aperture leading to the front door.

3. At Powis Castle, brick terraces are bounded by sculptured banks of yew, while in the foreground neat box edging encloses flower beds.

4/5/6. Fences made of simple painted palings give a delightful linear quality to the boundaries of small houses.

1

2

□ The most exciting element of a fence or hedge, or a wall, is its sense of continuity and of containing what you own or cultivate; and then the way it is pierced — by a simple opening with an arched head, or perhaps no top to it at all. With the gate or doorway, having it closed or left open leads the eye through to the space beyond. Successful gardens have variety of containment — long views, contrasting with small contained areas.

□ I am always looking for inspiration from other people's solutions when travelling around the countryside. If you are about to build a fence, or a wall, make a doorway, or plant a hedge, look and see what other people have done. For example, I was interested to see that the beech in the hedges at Drummond Castle are planted in a straight line only 5—6 inches apart, and are 16 feet high. There are so many infinite variations on a garden doorway; unfortunately, curves and pointed shapes are more expensive than straight lines, but are often worth the extra expense for the sense of visual interest they create.

1/2/3. Victorian cast-iron fences and gates work well with earlier houses, besides being practical.

3

Apertures

□ Apertures are extremely important in any garden design. A tall, narrow gap between hedges, an opening in a wall, the way through from one part of a garden to another lends excitement and drama to the atmosphere of the garden.

1

2

1. Dramatic arched opening in an ancient yew hedge provides an impressive vista.
2. A narrow gap in this Edwardian yew hedge provides an element of drama in Countess Beauchamp's garden.
3. I formed this gothic doorway in a barn to give access and a prospect on to a distant terrace in my own garden.

3

1. Wooden painted gates partly open at Hidcote.
2. Newly made gothic wrought iron gates lead to a swimming pool garden in the Vaucluse.
3. Early eighteenth-century wrought iron gate in Lord Tweedsmuir's garden.

4. Yew hedge pierced with wooden gateposts surmounted by carved baskets of flowers.

5. I pierced a wall in my garden to give access to a small garden beyond, and designed this simple spider's-web Chinese Chippendale softwood painted door.

6. In a magnificent curtain wall by Vanbrugh, a simple iron gate gives drama in the Earl of Ancaster's garden.

7. A cast iron trellis panelled doorway in Lady Caroline Gilmour's enchanting riverside garden leads into Syon Park.

8. A delightfully simple but stylish aperture in the outer part of the Somersets' garden in Gloucestershire.

9. A trellis gate hung from posts surmounted by wooden urns in Oxfordshire has great style.

□ The most obvious elements of gardens are the verticals — trees, tall plants, walls and hedges rising from the ground. But of equal importance are the horizontal areas, the expanse seen when sitting or standing in the garden or from the house. Too much mown grass or too many gravel paths can become monotonous. An excess of brick or flagstones can be arid and dead. As with the vertical elements of a garden, you must strive for variety in material and texture underfoot. What you use is going to be significant throughout the year, whatever the season.

□ Thyme planted between paving smells delicious underfoot. Aim for contrast, but not too much of it in designing your garden. Sir Edwin Lutyens was a master of garden design, and he considered with great care, every detail of the progression round a garden. Always consider what is on the ground.

1. At Chatsworth, slabs of stone provide a practical surface in winter, between splendid beech hedges, incorporating caryatids from Chiswick House.
2. At Hatfield House, cobbled treads and stone risers give a bold textural effect.
3. Random but large sections of stone form this romantic stairway in Provence.
4. The Marchioness of Salisbury created this path combining cobbles and irregular stone centrepieces at Cranborne Manor.
5. In my stable yard I have used washed gravel right up to the stone walls, but have left decisive planting areas edged neatly in wood.
6. John Mackenzie's garden at Saint-Jean, Cap Ferrat, has herring-bone brick edged with pebbles. It makes an interesting textural effect.

□ Change of level is also important, for it can break up a tedious flat expanse, and even under deep snow this is still effective. I like gravel paths and, with modern weed-killers, their upkeep is minimal. I know a number of people who reject the idea of a formal high-maintenance garden and achieve dramatic effect by having long grass, beautiful until mid July, coming almost up to the house, cutting mown paths around the perimeter, and, through the long grass, leading to a glade or opening. When it is cut there is only an awkward two-week interval while it becomes green again, and it can then be rewarding for the whole of the rest of the year.

□ Stone paths and terraces are ideal. It is possible to buy second-hand paving stones, often from town councils, but at considerable cost. However, there are many concrete paving stones available, which are quite acceptable. New textures and colours are being produced each year. I was lucky enough to find, under a thin layer of concrete in my backyard, several thousand cobblestones, which I have re-used to advantage as a border around my front door porch, on a geometric stone and cobblestone terrace and as the surround to the swimming pool. Second-hand cobbles can be bought, but it requires some skill to bed and lay them properly.

□ Before making decisions about your new garden underfoot, go and see some of the great small gardens that are open to the public, and the larger ones as well. Hidcote and Sissinghurst immediately spring to mind: see the various solutions that the great gardeners who created these found for the problems they faced — and which, in one form or another, you may face.

1. At Sissinghurst, looking from a slightly raised grass terrace edged in brick down on to a stone flag path also edged in brick, which is in turn edged in box.
2. Looking through the long double line of yew hedges to the rose-covered rotunda, again at Sissinghurst.
3/4. Brick and stone flagged paths, one edged severely in clipped box, with yew hedges, and the other enclosed with romantic planting.

□ Using gravel through areas of mown lawn, it is advisable to use treated wood as an edging to contain the gravel, and a foundation of cinders keeps it dry and solid. At Hatfield, Lady Salisbury has made some attractive paths of camomile, alternating with squares of stone between the flowerbeds; it smells delicious when you walk on it.

□ I enjoy using grass at different heights: tightly mown lawns, meeting what I call 'beard length' grass about four inches tall and then long grass.

□ Brick paths can be constructed of various different-coloured bricks although I prefer a single colour rather than a mixture. They can be laid in a number of different patterns, including herringbone, and laying the centre of the path longways, and the border bricks sideways.

□ A change of level in the garden, particularly in relation to the house, can be extremely successful. A slope can be left as a slope, but it can also with the help of a bulldozer be turned into a definite change of level; a stone or gravel terrace outside a French window leading from a drawing-room or a dining-room can be pleasing and practical. At all costs, avoid crazy paving, although stones or slabs need not be square. They can be of dissimilar size, provided they are all straight edged, and laid at right angles to each other.

1. Guildford Bell, in his Melbourne, Victoria, garden, used brick underfoot in a generous, stylish way.
2. Lord De L'Isle devised this bold use of silver ground cover under standard trees.
3. Looking down from the top of the mount at Kew Palace; covered in box, the winding path is made of square cut stones.

Sunken garden at Hampton Court, with a circular pond in the centre, in the formal style of the seventeenth century.

Textures

□ Some of the best gardens rely principally on texture
for their effect — on the contrast of a hard line of
flagstone with the softer but still sculptural lines of the
clipped hedges, or the delightful interplay of large leafed
plants with the smaller scale of box behind. Texture
should be designed into a garden. It can remain
constant throughout the year, or it may alter with the
seasons. The textures of bare branches against a winter
sky may be as striking and effective as full foliage in
spring and summer.

1

1. The lime tunnel at Hidcote in Gloucestershire which provides textural interest the year round.
2. In Christopher Lloyd's magical garden at Great Dixter in Sussex mown grass and long grass are used in a masterly way. In the long grass he has encouraged many charming wild flowers.

2

1. At Cock Road Farm John Stephanidis shows a fine sense of texture with the gravel paths, low box and taller planting of lavender.
2. A large walled garden, divided into huge beds containing fruit trees, vegetables and flowers, bordered with box, and grass paths edged with brick in Dorset.
3. Silver-leafed edging looks delightful in this yew-enclosed garden planted with grey-silver and almond-green colours, including two standard eucalyptus.

1

2

4

5

4. Detail of formal planting at Kew Palace, with box and silver-grey santolina.
5. In Rory Cameron's garden near Menerbes, his masterly use of texture is seen here with the contrast of washed gravel, planting and stone walls.
6. At Kew, cobblestones, box and grey planting provide superb and refined examples of textural contrast.

3

6

1. Variety of texture in planting provides tremendous
light and shade: euphorbia, seen here above a plant of
smaller habit, has excellent delineation.
2. This summer tapestry comprises hosta, iris, thistle,
and crambe against a yew hedge.

1

Textures

1. At La Chevre d'Or, Biot, a pebble path punctuates a variety of Mediterranean textures.
2. Splendid contrast provided by many different textural elements.
3. Clipped olive trees with a tailored hedge beneath, supported by a severe gravel path, make a perfect foil for the Mediterranean cypresses behind them.
4. Gunnera luxuriant by the lake at Syon Park.

5. Bold clump of euphorbia at Kelmscott.
6. An explosion of foxgloves naturalised under trees in Oxfordshire.
7. Yew and beech hedging in an exciting juxtaposition of textures at Hidcote.
8. Campanula and honeysuckle combining well on a June day in the west of England.

Light and shade

☐ Light and shade change through the day and through the year. They give drama and a sense of movement to the garden. There is nothing more attractive than strong sunlight bursting through an aperture in a dense, tall yew hedge. Arbours, walks, and tunnels which form a covered walk can provide a shady area which can be very welcome on a hot day. Light and shade are closely related to texture: light, loose leaves will show brightly against a dark surround or background hedge. Some leaves show a different colour when moved by the wind. In a year-round garden there is a strong dominance of green shades, and the contrast between light and dark gives the interest. A mundane garden is flat, with little in the way of contrast and surprise. It is the supreme test of a garden that it can work and be exciting with little more than a monochrome colour range; and some of the most thrilling gardens I know rely on a few simple effects — texture, contrast, light and shade. There is a wonderful sense of permanence in a garden like this, refined down to its essentials.
☐ Life in a hot climate demands a rather different attitude to planting. Shade is no longer merely an effect but essential, vital for the comfort of the house and enjoyable use of the garden. The same elements of contrast in foliage and mood still apply; but water now plays an overwhelmingly important part in the design of a successful garden in a hot climate. One of the most fascinating houses I know is the Villa Vizcaya in Florida, where John Deering created a classical Italian Renaissance garden layout in a mangrove swamp. At first sight one has the sensation of being outside Florence. But on closer inspection, all the formal bedding and the lines of trees are of varieties rarely seen in Europe. Deering achieved at Vizcaya, in the intense heat of the Florida sun, an overwhelming sense of shade from the light. He also provided one feature which is remarkably successful in a tropical or sub-tropical garden. He used the spoil from the excavations for the house, garden and the formal canals which are around it, to build a mount at the centre of the end of the main vista, rather like seventeenth-century English college gardens, and on a hot afternoon, if you climb up the thirty-foot staircase, there is a very evident and welcome drop in temperature.

An earthenware pot of good proportion provides a terminal point for this tunnel, which shows the effective contrast of light and shade.

Light and shade

1. The enchanting silver and white garden planted by Roderick Cameron and now owned by M. and Mme Pierre Schlumberger, is a fine example of light and shade achieved in the Mediterranean.
2. The Somersets' garden at The Cottage in Badminton was laid out with great style with the help of Russell Page.
3. This shady arbour terminates in a delicate garden seat.
4. At La Chèvre d'Or in the south of France, M. and Mme Champin have created a delightful open-air room, with walls of clipped olive, and superb grass making a delightful foil for the venerable pine tree.

5. An avenue of plane trees in Provence providing wonderful protection and shade from the strong wind and sun.

6. In Portugal, the Bramäo box garden was suffering through lack of water and extreme sunlight, so in the summer of 1981, Dom Luiz had this green hairnet suspended above it.

7. The Comte and Comtesse de Brantes have created a stylish and simple garden near Avignon.

8. A good example of light and shade produced by different textures and tall trees in the background of an English garden.

Gardening on the house

□ The use of the walls of a house for planting is of great antiquity, for it provided a warm and protected background for fruit, vines, climbing roses, jasmine, and other ornamental climbers. A great many houses, particularly those with little in the way of architectural distinction, depend for their appeal on the plants that cover them. At the other extreme of the spectrum, great architecture is sometimes overbearingly severe and cold. It can benefit tremendously from the delicate tracery of a Gloire de Dijon climbing rose carefully trained between columns and entablatures. Many a country cottage would look incomplete without a bower of honeysuckle over its porch, or groups of hollyhocks standing like sentinels on either side of its latticed windows. *Vitis coignetiae*, the decorative vine, can give great warmth and lushness to red brick or stone façades; in the city, hanging flower baskets, window boxes, and creepers, will give life to an otherwise dour exterior. I love controlled Virginia creeper. At Albany there is Ampelopsis growing up to twenty feet then hanging down very romantically.

□ The colour of the plants you choose — the rose or the clematis, the ceanothus, the japonica or wisteria — is important, depending on whether you have mellow red brick, colour wash, grey stone or stock brick, warm peach-coloured stone, modern hard engineering brick, rough shuttered concrete or painted weatherboarding. Of the roses on red brick walls, I like pinks — Albertine and Zéphirine Drouhin. On stone walls, Souvenir de la Malmaison, and other cream and pale pink strains. Equally satisfactory are yellow or creamy-yellow roses, like Lady Hillingdon, which flatter the colour of the stone. On a small severe modern house, vines give a marvellously warming effect, and even in winter their cobweb-like tentacles soften the silhouette. In contrast to this in another part of the façade of this sort of house, a carefully trained and clipped japonica can add an architectural element.

1. Nothing suits an old house with mullioned, leaded windows so well as a good creeper climbing on its walls, though great care must be taken to discipline it.
2. This side of the house belonging to my Swiss associate, Fleur Vulliod, is entirely clad in Virginia creeper. Under a balcony she stores vine prunings in a decorative way ready for winter fires.
3. Creeper trained in a most entrancing way on a pavilion at Packwood House in Warwickshire, totally complementary to the architectural details.

1

1. Magnolia luxuriating in a warm corner between walls at Hidcote.
2. At Shoreham, in Kent, where Samuel Palmer painted some of his most lyrical, romantic landscapes: a Victorian cottage has been partially wrapped in *Clematis montana*.

2

□ Modern houses, especially where there are a number of the same pattern grouped together, benefit greatly from a large textural planting at their base such as acanthus, berberis, phormium or choisya. Planting in relation to the house is exceptionally important, and when building a new house, or buying one in the process of being built, this should be envisaged and discussed with the architect or builder. Ideally, this should be at the very first sketch planning stage. You should have in mind from the outset whether you want a romantic, random planting, or whether it is to be an extension of the architectural feel of the house itself in the form of much more geometric planting. Notice how old houses and old gardens are always beautifully related: a good and successful garden, however new, will always have the sense of this harmony.

1. A stone house in Oxfordshire beautifully complemented by enchanting climbing roses.
2. This cottage in Little Haseley has the perfect cottage garden and a romantic abundance of things growing on its façade.
3. Wisteria effectively muting the aggressive nineteenth-century baroque gate piers to the walled gardens at Harlaxton Manor in Lincolnshire.
4. The severe classical lines of Sutton Park are softened at ground level with sympathetic planting.
5. This undistinguished cottage at Ewelme has been given distinction by the planting on the façade.
6. In Badminton village, climbing Peace blends beautifully with the buff stone and cream paint work on this cottage.

Colour

☐ Colour can make or mar a garden. I know of many small gardens with an exquisite use of colour, depending on a delightful co-ordination of salmon pinks, pale-blue pinks, silver leaves, even a touch of lemon yellow; I can also think of others which are hideous beyond belief, with raucous reds and screaming oranges, and unnaturally brilliant blues. Getting colour right in the garden is very similar to a good sense of colour in interior design. It is a question of training your eye and seeing how other people's colour combinations please or displease you. Be selective and discerning. A very safe way of achieving a successful colour combination is of having, as I have advocated for interiors, colour themes. All yellows and pale oranges and greens go together, reds, pinks and oranges go together, and all whites, blues and greens work well together. I know of several gardens with flower beds of different yellows, apricots, oranges and creams; this makes a very attractive effect — a complete mass of all different blue and mauve flowers can be very effective. A colour theme such as yellow and pale orange makes an enormous impact, and can be composed of all sorts of different annuals, shrubs, and plants, giving a great variety of texture, height, and habit. A room which has no colour theme or colour scheme is a mess: a garden which has not had serious thought about colour is equally unattractive.

☐ There is nothing more pleasing to me than all-green gardens with a wide range of contrasting greens: grass, yew, box, beech, hornbeam, ivy-covered walls, laurel, making a delightful green theme. The plants within such a garden would be those that one grows entirely for textural interest, not for their flowers. I know certain gardeners who grow some plants exclusively for their leaves and texture, and abhor the flowers, nipping them off when they are about to bloom.

John Fowler planted these two lines of hornbeam in 1947 in his garden at Odiham. I first saw this garden in the early 1950s and it had an overwhelming influence on my garden thinking.

In Paris the Baronne Geoffroi de Waldener trained,
with loving care, this elephant made of box in the all-
green part of her garden.

Mr Basil Feilding's father planted this triumph of topiary in Oxfordshire in 1924.

Mrs Claude Lancaster's garden in Oxfordshire burgeons with luxuriant green walks, topiary and arbours.

☐ The colour of your doors, gates, and even your wheelbarrow should be carefully considered; I favour dark green as a paint colour for doors, tubs and seats. White-painted garden furniture has to me become associated with the obvious, especially since so many pieces of garden furniture are now made or covered in an unpleasant white plastic, but give consideration to buffs and beiges and other subtle colours for use in the garden. If you do not want to assume the burden of regular repainting, use a wood such as cedar for seats, fences and gates, which becomes a beautiful silver colour with weathering.

☐ Although I have seen some successful all-white, or white-and-silver gardens, I find they are a little hackneyed, but if you are going to do one then do it with considerable courage and a generous sense of scale.

Design in a small garden is even more important than in a medium or large one, because space is limited and the planning and selection of plants must be faultless. Similarly, it must be attractive at all times of year, simply because it will all be seen, all the time, at a glance. In any small garden I would want to have a *Magnolia grandiflora*, two Constance Spry roses, herbs and an arrangement of formally planted trees which would be clipped. On the house, I would choose japonica, choisya, some climbing roses, and nearby two large clumps of hellebores, with their leaves looking good all year round. I would grow bulbs in tubs, which would be replaced with pelargoniums. Bulbs take up a lot of space in a small garden and look untidy for quite a long while after flowering. One of the great advantages of a small garden is that you can water all of it regularly, much more easily than a large garden. You can even have a built-in sprinkler system, operated on a time mechanism. Remember that a small garden, with its concentrated use of soil, is going to need far more feeding than a larger area, particularly in city atmospheres.

1. Mr Hardy Amies' Oxfordshire garden: four ball-topped obelisks sitting on ball feet dominate in a most stylish and effective way his box-edged flower-filled geometric garden.
2. Roderick Cameron adapted this Chinese Chippendale fence and gate for a small corner of his garden, and used a splendidly overscaled pottery container for a palm tree under a vigorous fig.
3. Profuse planting of a small corner against rusticated plaster work achieving maximum textural interest.

1 Contained planting of flowers in a carefully clipped geometric garden.
2. In a small garden, an oil tank can be exceptionally obtrusive; but Mrs Lees-Milne skilfully hides hers with trellis on which she grows a luxuriant honeysuckle.
3. A tiny plot by the roadside on the outskirts of Villandry reflects the great garden down the road. A row of potatoes in front of a row of arum lilies makes a sublime contrast.
4/5. Two corners of a minute garden in the village of Gordes in Provence demonstrate concentrated use of space and pot gardening in the sun to good effect.

1. A small city garden, photographed before I suggested alterations — incredibly simple: a square column made of concrete raising an existing rather pleasing bust to the height for which it was originally intended, and changing the contour of the planting to a more interesting shape.
2. Two lines of standard rose bushes flank the three lines of irregular but straight-edged flagstones leading to the front door of Kelmscott Manor.

3. Superb contrast of textures in a small French garden.
4. In her large *small garden* Alvilde Lees-Milne created an enchanting border avoiding all the obvious plants.
5. Penelope Hobhouse uses containers creatively for small plants on a low terrace wall, while making an interesting contrast of scale between the succulents in them, the tall feathery lavender, and the mass of the box, which leads away from the fine seventeenth-century house.

□ Small gardens usually suffer from close neighbours, but trellis to give height and privacy can be clad in delicious honeysuckle and clematis, which during the summer will give shade to the house next door, and in winter, when bare, will allow the light your neighbours will want. Do not fight your neighbour but try to make peace from the moment you move in, and arrive at planting solutions which will benefit you both. For a small house or bungalow, the garden is an extension of the house, and provides yet another living space, and therefore some form of garden shelter, a pavilion or summerhouse, so that you can use the garden even in the rain, is a great advantage. In these gardens, plants in tubs or containers can be used to give much quicker results than normal planting, and by building up beds

A simple scheme for a small awkwardly-shaped garden behind a terraced house. Creeper architecturally controlled can give great character to an unassuming house.

with brick or boarded containers in terraces, you can get greater differences of height immediately. In a small town garden, it is usually a waste of time having grass, because it hardly justifies a good lawnmower, and is very time consuming: gravel, stone and brick can make an extremely pleasing terrace or central path. Small gardens need durable surfaces to withstand constant use.

☐ Small country gardens should not be grand or pretentious, but a double line of apple trees can give a nice sense of architectural gardening even in the smallest area. The great charm of cottage gardens is when they are full of every kind of flower, vegetable and fruit, all grown together, mixed up in a delightfully rich and random way.

A strong garden plan can transform the most pedestrian plot and careful planting can transform the most utilitarian building, especially if a period detail is added to the fenestration.

A Greek tomb-inspired porch supporting climbing roses and a two-tiered plant stand give character to this basically simple geometrically laid out garden incorporating traditional garden planting. Ugly boundary fences are quickly camouflaged by creepers.

virginia creepers

gooseberries

simple greek tomb inspired wooden stand to support cli. rose.

wild strawberries

BOX

BOX

Gravel

BAY trees

veg

Flowers

← Brick divisions

chives

Lavender

This stark situation needs a strong decisive attitude. Privacy and character can be acquired by planting hedges, climbing roses and by adding shutters and building a rustic arbour at the end of the drive. Beech is very quick growing if well fed.

□ Maximum utilisation of space is vital. Instead of a strawberry bed, grow strawberries in window boxes attached in rows to a wall, leaving ground space free for other things. Gooseberries grown as standard bushes allow for planting underneath. Runner beans and sweet peas can be grown up trellis obelisks. I advocate vertical gardening in a very small space. If you have an empty rectangular back garden, why not have a terrace immediately outside the living room, and then a third of the way down the garden build a wall with an interesting aperture. It need not have a gate — it could be a wall with an opening and two finials, and beyond, in different mood, a different type of planting. This will give you the feeling of having two gardens rather than one, each moderately private from the other. The division can be fencing, or trellis, both clad with plants, or a hedge. A pergola, with a vine or rose growing on it, would create the same effect. A large, overscaled garden ornament can make a garden seem much bigger than it is, providing a surprise in scale.

2

1. Looking down on Mr Egerton's small garden, one sees how all the available space has been used, extending beyond the garden wall on to a narrow bed alongside the pavement, giving pleasure both to his neighbours and the public.

2. A detailed view of the planting in this garden.

3. For this extremely small London back garden, I would make a definite statement, with a line of six pleached and clipped hornbeam trees. The planting behind them would be with rhubarb and rheum, and the underplanting of the front with hostas. I would use a number of plants in flower pots and would break up the rather ordinary, concrete slab paving by making a panel of cobblestones.

4. For a small city garden I have devised this scheme of a solid beech hedge at the back with two clumps of choisya, punctuated by an openwork wooden trellis with ivy or a vine growing round it. It must be controlled sufficiently for the basic lines of the obelisk to be the focal point. A rectangular basin of water surrounded by flagstones is balanced by two flowerbeds.

4

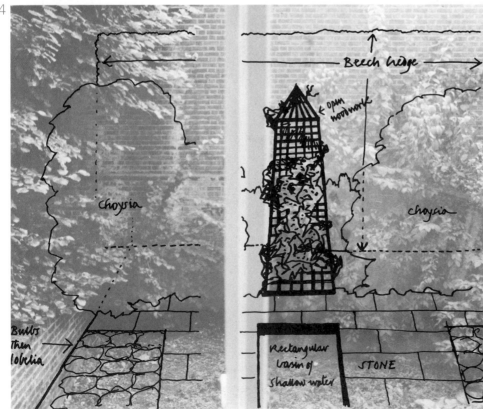

Beech hedge

open woodwork

choysia

choysia

Bulbs then lobelia

Rectangular basin of shallow water

STONE

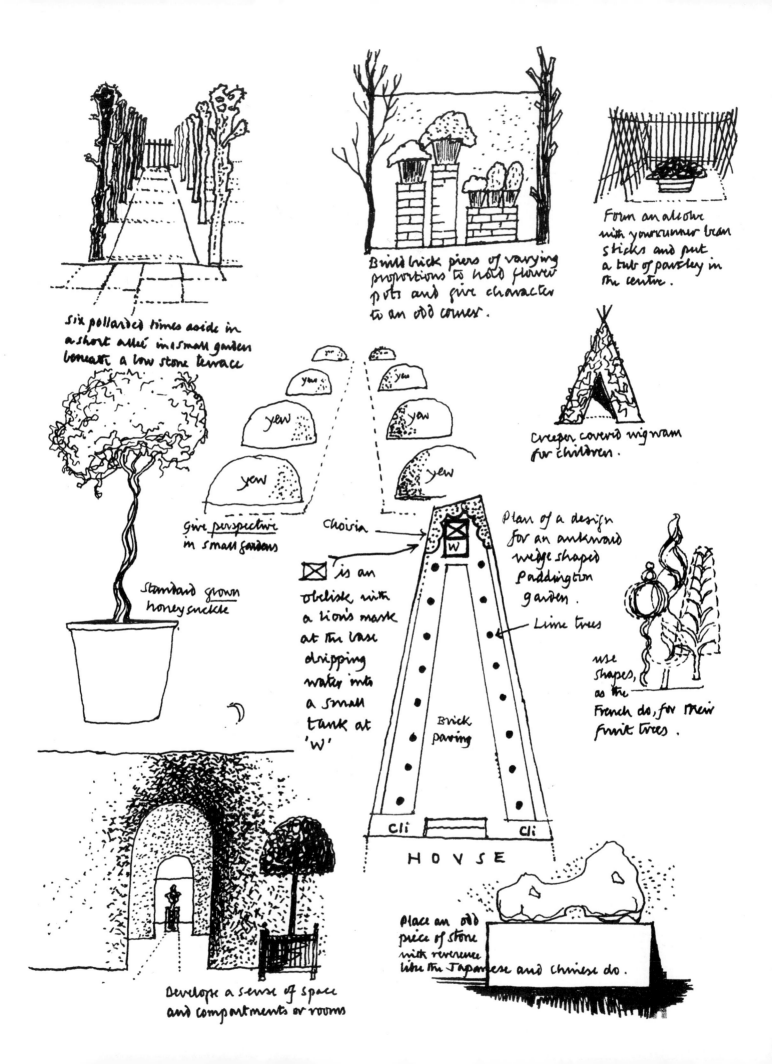

Six pollarded limes aside in a short allée in a small garden beneath a low stone terrace

Build brick piers of varying proportions to hold flower pots and give character to an odd corner.

Form an alcove with your runner bean sticks and put a tub of parsley in the centre.

Give perspective in small gardens

Creeper covered wigwam for children.

Standard grown honeysuckle

Choisia

⊠ is an obelisk with a lion's mask at the base dripping water into a small tank at 'W'

Plan of a design for an awkward wedge shaped Paddington garden.

Lime trees

Brick paving

Cli   Cli

H O V S E

use shapes, as the French do, for their fruit trees.

Develope a sense of space and compartments or rooms

Place an old piece of stone with reverence like the Japanese and Chinese do.

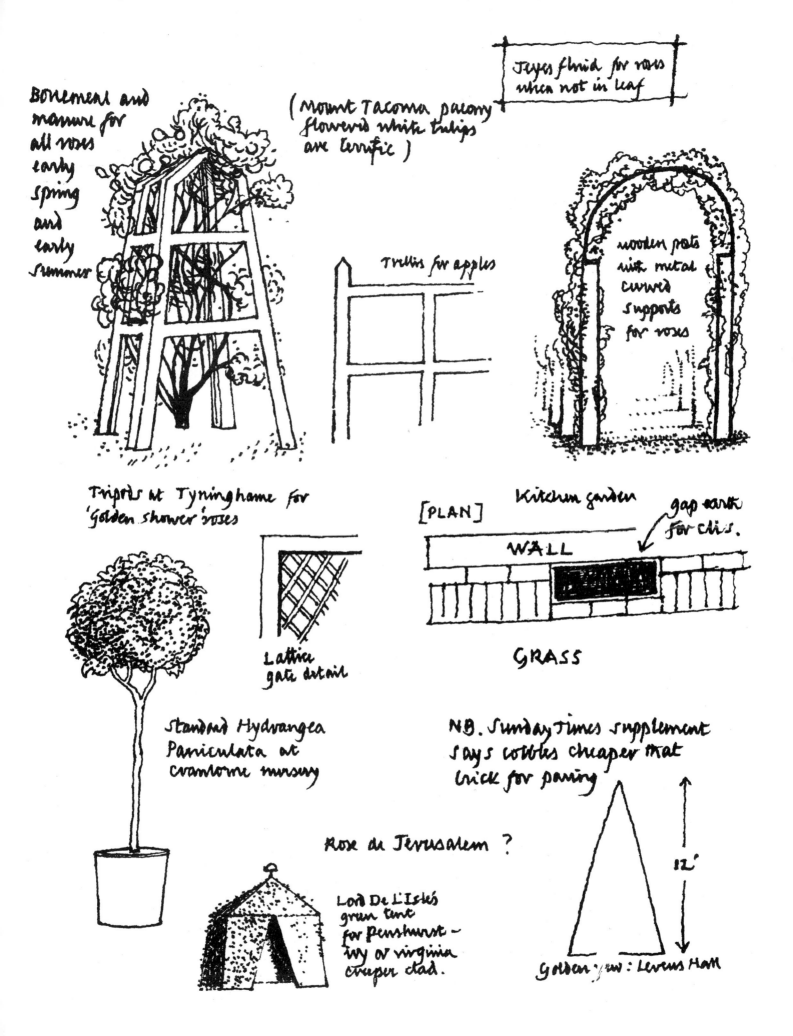

Bonemeal and manure for all roses early spring and early summer

(Mount Tacoma paeony flowered white tulips are terrific)

Jeyes fluid for roses when not in leaf

Trellis for apples

wooden posts with metal curved supports for roses

Tripods at Tyninghame for 'Golden shower' roses

Lattice gate detail

Kitchen garden
[PLAN]

gap earth for clis.

WALL

GRASS

Standard Hydrangea Paniculata at cranborne nursery

NB. Sunday Times supplement says cobbles cheaper that brick for paving

Rose de Jerusalem?

Lord De L'Isle's green tent for Penshurst – ivy or virginia creeper clad.

12'

Golden yew: Levens Hall

Small gardens

1. Mr and Mrs David Lawman's garden, behind their Eaton Terrace house, circa 1820, has as its main feature a hundred-year-old weeping oak, the only one in London. Impatiens and geraniums provide splashes of colour in the delightfully shaded garden.

2. At Albany, neatly clipped privet hedges make a disciplined background for tubs, alternately planted with variegated laurel and rhododendrons on either side of the Rope Walk.

3. A gothicised house on the Thames at Syon has been clothed in fig trees.

4/5. Mrs Derek Vernon-Wentworth's London garden, which I designed in 1959. I planted a row of lime trees, pleached to follow the shape of the garden. On the main façade, I suggested an ample window box filled with petunias.

☐ Most city gardens and small cottage gardens can be made infinitely more interesting at relatively low cost by changing dramatically the level of containers for planting. I know a small garden in Sydney where the area behind the house is very limited, and a dramatic effect has been achieved by building a high wall halfway back in the garden, with a steep flight of steps in the middle. The plants on the higher level are almost like full-grown trees when viewed from the dining-room and then looking back at the house from the higher level, the lower part – the well – has been filled with a variety of containers, of different sizes and shapes, creating a good up-and-down profile of planting within a small area which is extremely effective. The same effect can be achieved by massing containers at different heights against an existing wall.

☐ I think small gardens need a sense of design even more than medium or large gardens, since the range of possible effects is more limited. But a well-thought-out city or suburban garden can be extremely pleasing. A small piece of water can give great life and interest, all year round. Many plants thrive in an urban atmosphere (which tends to be warmer than the country) and any which do not can be helped by good feeding. The warmth also prolongs the active life of plants: they come into leaf earlier.

1/2/3/4. Francis Egerton's London garden is perhaps even more splendid outside his boundaries than within. The delightful early nineteenth-century house has a welcoming pair of bay trees and a severe yet stylish black and white canvas awning. To the right of it, a splendid healthy specimen of *Magnolia grandiflora*. Within the garden, lilies grown in pots have their own sunblind, here seen raised, but which can be lowered to stop them going over too soon or drying out.

3

□ I designed a small garden in Belgravia for a client, planting a row of lime trees which I pleached following the contour of the property. I gravelled the main area and put two terracotta urns planted abundantly with geraniums in the summer and evergreens in the winter. For a small wedge-shaped garden in Paddington Basin, I advised my clients to cover the central part with flagstones and brick and to plant two lines of trees converging at the tip of the triangle on an obelisk, from which water fell into a small square basin. Because the point of the garden is furthest from the house, the trees are going away in false perspective, making the garden seem twice as long as it really is, and the eye is forced towards the obelisk which is the focal point. Petunias will be massed at the foot of the trees in summer. In contrast with this rather ordered geometrical approach which I prefer, I know of some small wild romantic gardens in London, where the profusion of shrubs, trees and flowers have great magic and a sense of protection from neighbours.

□ Walls and fences are often essential to hide an oil tank or perhaps a neighbour's unsightly garden shed. Open-spaced brick walls, wooden trellis, and hedges can be invaluable. Climbers such as honeysuckle can be trained up over trellis partitions to good effect.

□ Every garden benefits from a small building, covered seat or a small folly, especially if well placed at the end of a vista or line of trees. It need not be elaborate, and can easily be constructed by the amateur.

□ Sun blinds and awnings can give character and atmosphere to houses, but remember the choice of the canvas or fabric is extremely important, and must relate to the colour of the house and the plants around it. Shiny plastic awnings and floral designs are, to me, totally unacceptable.

4

Perspective

☐ Perspective leads the eye from the house to the horizon or, in a small town roof garden, or indeed in a cottage garden, from the interior to the furthest point over which you have control. In practice, in a minute area, this sense of perspective may consist of six tubs, three on either side of a central path leading to a garden gate, or possibly some garden ornament. But even in these few feet perspective can help to achieve style. Perspective gives a sense of relative scale — those things which are closest to you naturally appear larger. But false scale and false perspective can also be employed. In a tiny backyard in southern France, I was faced with the problem that the site was small and irregular in shape. I wanted it to look longer than it was, so I planted trees on each side following the narrowing shape of the site and the distance between the trees decreasing, so that the eye was completely tricked.

☐ The grandest example of the use of perspective is undoubtedly the gardens of Versailles. The great vista from the Galerie des Glaces, the most resplendent reception room in Europe, down over the two basins to the canal at the end, had great influence on gardens all over the world. It was the apex of grand formal gardening and no subsequent ruler or millionaire has ever come anywhere close to the conception of Le Nôtre and Louis XIV.

☐ Yet the principles are essentially those understood by any artist, and I suspect that my fascination with perspective stems from my time as an art student. At one time English gardening was preoccupied with lines, as you can see in the bird's-eye views by Kip of early eighteenth-century layouts, with their almost ceaseless repetition of avenues, walks, pleached *allées* and contained areas for different purposes — vegetables, fruit, flowers, fowls, grazing and so on. Much of this was lost when Capability Brown swept aside earlier designs, to provide the great parks that we know today. If in the past formality and geometry was overdone, later too little attention was paid to the virtues of this style in gardens. Now that gardens are much smaller, the advantages of a more formal, designed approach are very much more evident.

With great boldness and sense of scale, this lime walk through the middle of a large walled garden in Dorset was planted ten years ago.

1. David Mlinaric, in his Norfolk garden, built a simple architectural rustic pergola, on which he is training old roses. Stylish and attractive the year round, it would give structure to any garden.
2. At Montacute, age-old yews illustrate a dramatic use of perspective.

□ By careful use of perspective, design, and very deliberate planting you can create the illusion of a much more extensive area. It should not be forgotten how incredibly labour-intensive many of the gardens in the style of Gertrude Jekyll were then, and are now, even with labour-saving devices.

□ Perspective in garden design requires careful and sensitive handling. Remember that when you are halfway down a walk, what you see to either side, and when looking back, must look as well as what you view from the main vantage point. At Versailles whether you are at the top, the middle or the bottom of the vast garden, the quality and the design around the great central vista are equally good. One useful idea, therefore, is to place ornaments or plants to either side of your main axis or vista which may not even be seen from the house, but which will give other focal points when you are halfway down. At Villandry, there is a great sense of perspective, but not orientated on the château itself, so you only grasp the principles on which it works once you are standing within the garden. This can be applied delightfully in a modern garden as a surprise, which appears as one thing from the house, and a much more complex and interesting set of shapes from close to.

1

2

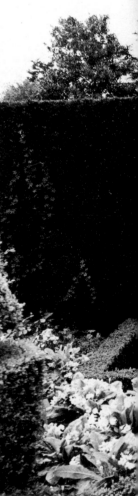

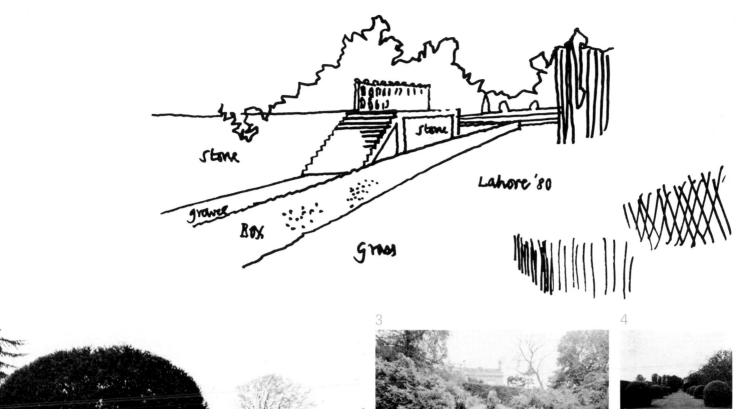

stone

stone

graves

Box

Grass

Lahore '80

3

4

1. Harold Nicholson and Vita Sackville-West were decisive garden planners and planters; this central yew *allée* is of exceptional length and effectiveness, yet it dates only from the early 1930s.

2. One of the many compartments or rooms at Hidcote, showing an interesting change in scale in the stone paving.

3. At Kiftsgate, a delightful walk, framed on either side by *Rosa mundi*.

4. At Penshurst Place, ancient clipped yews — yew shapes in front of yew hedges — give a sense of perspective.

1. At Madresfield Court, quadruple lines of poplars border a garden drive.

2/3/4/5. Two Dorset gardens and one in
Gloucestershire show good examples of the use of
perspective. Here is not only the technique of the
straight path disappearing into the distance, but the use
of a distant focus, as it terminates with a pot, a seat,
another avenue, or an obelisk.

The year-round garden

☐ The most successful gardens are those which are pleasing all through the year. To achieve this plant evergreens, lines of trees, create topiary, in an architectural, design-conscious way. The flowering season of the majority of plants is at most four weeks, and therefore it is essential to choose a number of plants like choisya and hellebores, bergenia, lavender, ivy and box, which are able through being evergreen, together with beech hedging, which retains its leaf, to contribute to the overall composition all through the year. This is one of the great disadvantages of the herbaceous border. Many shrubs and trees are as attractive in winter as in summer. When deciding on the design and planting for your garden, remember, besides the four glorious months of summer, the other eight.

1

2

□ *Iris stylosa* is a very slow thing to get established. It needs to be on rather poor stony soil, and loves the warmth of a south facing wall. If you are patient, this charming, winter-flowering iris will bear you endless crocus-like buds, which picked before they open will last for a day or two indoors, and have a delicious spring scent in the most depressing months of winter. It blooms from early December until late March. A bud brought into the house and put into warm water will open in two hours. But there are many other autumn, winter, and early spring-flowering plants and shrubs.

□ Another excellent evergreen, which clips well, is *Phillyrea augustifolia*, which is a useful alternative to yew or box.

1. In the garden at Easton Neston in Northamptonshire this cedar dates from the first planting in the early eighteenth century. The garden was altered and elaborated in the 1920s, and is a perfect example of a garden that looks magnificent the year round.
2. Dom Luiz Bramão's garden in the Algarve has the maximum of year-round planting — olives, pittosporum, cypress, lavender, and many things grown in pots which are decorative in winter as well as in summer.
3. HRH The Princess of Hesse and the Rhine's courtyard at Wolfsgarten has a stunning planting of plane trees, which are as beautiful in winter as in summer, on account of their severe pollarding.

3

3

1. A small evergreen parterre planted by Mr Roderick Cameron at Saint-Jean, Cap Ferrat, is full of enchantment.
2. Parallel lines of lime trees are terminated with a Chinese Chippendale gate in Countess Munster's Oxfordshire garden.
3. Countess Munster, a great gardener, planted Bampton with enormous style. The standard rose bushes give dramatic height: there are four matching corner beds in this part of the square garden.
4/5. Lady Gibbs planned this delightful rose arcade in her garden. In another part of it, a rustic pergola provides splendid year-round architecture and perspective.
6. The late Lord Faringdon planted this handsome architectural yew hedge to conceal his swimming pool at Buscot Park, owned by the National Trust.

6

☐ Containers can contribute a great deal to garden design. I like to use a pair of tubs on either side of a doorway, or a pair of large flowerpots on either side of an opening in a hedge. I also like to see pots massed together, all different shapes and sizes containing different annuals or bedding plants. It is amusing to collect them, and a wide variety can be found, both new and old. A number of modern potters are producing attractive designs in terracotta, and almost anything can be pressed into service as an effective container. It is a mistake to use them sparingly, or too discreetly. Containers should make a statement as to where they are and what they contain: used well, they can provide focal points within a garden that, unlike so many elements of a garden, can be moved or adjusted. When locating a container, I spend a great deal of time propping it up on breeze blocks, or moving it from place to place until I have it exactly right, a time-consuming exercise but worthwhile if they are to make a proper impact.

Good earthenware pots at the Cranborne Garden Centre in Dorset.

A row of flowerpots with different plants growing in them gives interest to a shady corner in a garden in Provence.

I grow nicotiana in great clumps, in large dark-green painted circular tubs.

1. A splendid nineteenth-century Versailles tub originally at Blenheim Palace.
2. Circular tub outside John Fowler's Hunting Lodge in Hampshire contains a circular cut box tree of great charm.
3. In their all-green garden, Mr and Mrs Feilding allow colour only in pairs of pots by doorways and openings in hedges.

4. At La Celle les Bordes near Paris, the Duchesse de Brissac has four pyramids of bay in these classical square containers on either side of the main doorway of her house.

5. On either side of my trellis porch in the country, I place tubs with standard gooseberry bushes in them in the summer.

4

5

1

☐ There are a number of containers you can make yourself. Modern Versailles tubs, brick planters, or straight sided plant holders of concrete which can be painted. Hollow sections of a fallen tree can be utilised. You can collect old kitchen sinks, chimney pots, and Victorian pottery tubs and urns. It is not what you use, but how you use it.

1. Containers of good proportion can add greatly to the character of gardens large and small. Here orange trees are growing in Florentine terracotta pots in a garden of box, lavender, and white begonias at Saint Jean, Cap Ferrat.
2. This old kitchen sink makes a delightful container for miniature plants, and forms with the other flower pots a pleasing arrangement which anybody can achieve.

2

1. The Dowager Lady Camoys used this stylish container, which is quite modern, with effect in a corner of her garden in Stonor.
2/3. In his new garden in Provence, Roderick Cameron has used two large Florentine pottery vases and planted them with speckled laurel, and in a newly planted box garden, an old stone urn makes a fine centrepiece.
4. I grow giant sunflowers in these simple wooden tubs and they flank the steps to the back door of my house.
5. Wanting to give a pair of vases more importance, I placed them on two brick piers, and surrounded them with bergenia.
6. An old jar creates interest in a corner of a romantic garden.

The distinguished interior decorator, John Fowler,
designed two similar but not matching pavilions, to be
seen halfway down the vista from his eighteenth-
century Gothic folly in Hampshire. Curved romantic
lines make a splendid contrast with the rigid clipped
rows of hornbeams.

☐ Garden pavilions are a vast subject but I have photographed some elaborate ones which could be adapted in much simplified form, and some unpretentious ones, including one of four matching pavilions I designed twenty-five years ago for Belgrave Square.

☐ The siting of utilitarian things (tool shed, greenhouse and compost heap), must be as carefully considered as that of ornamental garden buildings and the planting of trees and shrubs. A garden building can be the important focal point just as a church spire can be an eyecatcher in a landscape. In my new garden the tool shed and greenhouse were the first to be considered.

1

1/2. My neighbour, Nancy Lancaster, built this delightful trellis pavilion as the centrepiece to her large walled garden. From without and within, it is full of charm, and it is exactly in scale to the size of the garden.

3. This French garden pavilion has many elements to learn from. Its solid roof has a most attractive pitch, a fine top finial, and a delightfully elaborate nineteenth-century cut wooden pelmet under the eaves. It is partially covered with clematis and Virginia creeper.

4. In the middle of Lady Caroline Somerset's fruit and vegetable garden is a delicate openwork pavilion, surmounted by a *Rosa banksiae*.

5. This garden building placed in the corner of the walled garden of Kelmscott Manor probably predates William Morris.

6. Mr Alistair McAlpine is an inveterate collector and in front of his stylish fruit cage is part of his collection of pottery cloches.

2

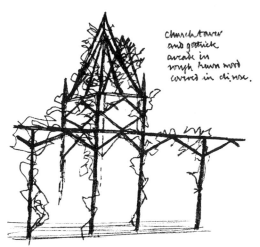

Church tower
and gothick
arcade in
rough hewn wood
covered in chinese.

3

4

5

6

☐ Of the mass-produced greenhouses, aluminium is the most practical, but I myself prefer painted or natural wood ones because they are more congenial to the other elements in a garden. Masterpieces of greenhouse design were constructed in the last century, and many still survive. Some of the details – devices on the corners and ribs, fretwork and filigree on the roof-line – can be adapted to give today's greenhouse more character. I never erect a wooden cover for Calor gas cylinders without considering carefully the design and proportion, and a useful garden shed can have character and style simply by adding a pretty porch or a circular window. The colour of wood or paint should be carefully thought out. Choose one colour for all your garden paintwork. I chose very very dark green. Off-white, beige and dark blue are good alternatives.

1

1. Knole: this delightful Regency pavilion overlooks
Lord Sackville's swimming pool.
2. The garden of the King of Sweden at Ulriksdahl;
this early nineteenth-century openwork trellis pavilion
of Gothic-Moorish design, could be the starting point
for a simplified version for use today.

2

☐ There are endless variations in old gardens to draw from. There are classical, chinese, gothick, rustic, neo-classic and baroque themes in the form of bridges, temples, orangeries, vineries, peach houses, dairies, rotundas, pagodas, 'umbrellos', covered seats, grottoes, arcades, game larders, tea houses, gazebos, in the great and small gardens the world over — all with a motif, style or conception to inspire us for garden buildings of today. My favourites are a small Moroccan pavilion at Eze-sur-Mer, a large elegant white marble and smoked glass pool pavilion at Retford Park in New South Wales, the Elizabethan brick gazebo at Long Melford Hall in Suffolk, and my own trellis arbour which I am building at present by the tennis court.

1/2. The Duchess of Rutland has recently created a spring garden below this Regency rustic pavilion, formed of natural knotted shapes.
3. The American Museum in Britain, near Bath, contains a reproduction of the 'schoolhouse' where George Washington taught his step-grandchildren geography at Mount Vernon. It sits charmingly among mixed borders.
4. In Mrs. van Roosmalen's garden, at Rekem in Belgium, there is a delightful pavilion enclosing a seat. This green structure is *Cornus mas*.
5. John Stephanidis, the interior designer, drew this splendid dovecote and had it built by casual labour.
6. One of four pavilions which I designed for the garden committee in Belgrave Square in the late 1950s.

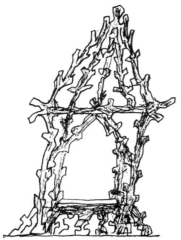

3

4

5

6

1. The elaborate series of canals on different levels
which descend from Buscot House into the lake at this
splendid National Trust property.
2. At the Château de Brantes water and trees have been
used to give a delightful perspective in the garden of
this beautiful house, of which the view has been
sacrificed to the misguided over-development of the
Provençal countryside.
3. My first love for water as an ingredient of a country
house was invoked by the formal canal at The Temple,
Stoke by Nayland, which I rented as a young man.
Flanked by magnificent trees, it was a source of endless
fascination.

Water

□ Of all the elements in gardening water is probably the most significant, from the hot dusty plains of Rajahstan where the Moguls made the most ingenious use of water ever conceived by mankind to the smallest suburban back garden where a simple jet in a small pond can produce a romantic atmosphere: water delights us in any garden. People lucky enough to have a natural pond, lake or stream are, of course, in a totally different league. I myself live on rather dry high ground although I am actively regenerating an old horse pond — an absolutely vital element of pre-tractor farming. I will have a limited number of water-loving plants — *Gunnera manicata*, for example — but used in a very natural way:

it is not going to be a botanical collection of water-loving plants. I have also used an old stone tank with a fine spout of water falling into it which is worked by a small electric pump re-cycling the water.

☐ If you are able to create even the smallest pond, you can indulge in all the delights of the aqua plant world and of those foliage plants such as gunnera and other moisture-loving foliage plants.

☐ Water provides life and movement in any garden, an element which is essentially satisfying, and a natural point of focal interest. I am not very keen on bog or water gardens in areas where they do not occur naturally. They can look very artificial.

1. In 1955, I planted pleached lines of hornbeam to left and right of The Temple and restored the eighteenth-century canal which had become quite silted up during the war.

2. The Bath of Diana at Penshurst Place in Kent. A splendid rectangular piece of water with a background of yew, and the ancient house and church beyond it.

2

1. The great canal at Chatsworth in Derbyshire, with
the emperor Fountain designed by Paxton for the visit of
the Czar of All the Russias is perhaps the greatest
example of a man-made piece of water in Great Britain.
The present Duke planted the splendid pleached limes
in 1952.
2. In total contrast, a minute back-garden pond,
beautifully planted, stocked with fish, and looking
inviting in the early summer sunlight. It demonstrates
that water can be a sublime quality in any man's garden.

At home in the country, I constructed this rusticated arch with a lion's head spilling water into a simple stone drinking trough. Knapped flint combines attractively with hostas in pots.

The Marchioness of Salisbury at Hatfield has adorned an existing fountain in a circular pond with superb planting in this square garden with its foil of trees.

The Baronne Geoffroi de Waldener recently completed part of her garden in Provence with this marine mask from which trickles a gentle flow of water into a mediaeval rectangular container from which the water spills, in turn, into a large tank below.

At Chatsworth, the water bubbles up in a rhythmic flow from the centre of a large basin.

1. An outer canal at Villandry, well clad in water lilies.
2. A basin of water in Portugal with a profusion of water lilies in a garden near Monchique.
3. The new water garden at Cranborne Manor.
4/5/6. At Shute Mr Michael and Lady Anne Tree have arum lilies growing in tubs in the canal. In the beech hedge on one side is a balcony, projecting over the water, with a very simple Chippendale fretted wooden design. The cascade, which in the Chinese manner, strikes musical chords, was designed for them by the renowned landscape architect, Sir Geoffrey Jellicoe.

☐ Swimming pools are a much neglected element from the point of view of really contributing to the garden design. Most people are inclined to think that swimming pools must be aquamarine blue and must be free-form in shape and only seen when the sky is blue, so they tend to be hidden behind ill-conceived rows of hideous macrocarpa hedging. I boldly placed my swimming pool 8 feet wide by 38 feet long 40 feet from my dining-room window and made it the central focal point of that particular side of my garden. I must add that I have painted it black so that it does not in any way look like a heated, filtered pool; it looks like a formal piece of water. Aggressive but practical chrome steps are demountable and only put out for bathing weather. Confronted by the usual lack of imagination or sense of design by the pool contractor, I have clothed the white plastic covers to the filtration units with loose cobblestones, which look all part of the 12-inch band of cobbles set in a weak mixture of concrete which edges the reconstituted stone paving pool surround.

1/2. The pool at The Cottage, Badminton, which cannot be seen from the house, even from the bedrooms, because of its clever placing and well-designed yew hedge. The pool has a natural cement finish and the volume of water produces a delightful grey-green colour. One side of the pool area is planted with white flowers and the result is one of the best swimming pool treatments in England.
3. At La Bastide du Roi, near Antibes, an amazing swimming pool: square with obelisks at each corner and a white marble figure reclining on a *chaise-longue* under a semi circular arch. It is sited immediately below the centre of the house.
4. John Mackenzie's swimming pool at Saint-Jean, Cap Ferrat, has superb datura plants all around it, and great simplicity.
5. This formal basin of water constructed a few years ago at Kew Palace gives a splendid idea for a swimming pool; the central feature has water descending from it into the pool.

3

4

5

☐ In an irregularly shaped, small garden in France, the widest part being by the house, I constructed a swimming pool which followed the shape of the garden, with the furthest end being narrower than the nearest end, and through false perspective, it made the swimming pool seem twice as long as it was in actuality.

☐ Site your pool carefully, out of the cold NE winds, surround it with beech hedges, a wall, or clipped trees, though not close to the pool. Leave plenty of space for sunbathing, and house the heating unit—compressed air heating is the latest and least expensive — carefully hidden behind a pool pavilion or in a nearby building.

☐ Natural cement with the volume of the water produces a subtle colour, and dark blue or green can be sympathetic in northern climates, whilst white is effective in the Mediterranean and tropical regions.

1

2

1. My own swimming pool is black, surrounded by reconstituted stone and cobblestones. It is intended to look like a formal pond, bordered by clipped chestnuts, and in the centre of the main vista.
2. A pool which I redesigned for M. and Mme Schlumberger at Saint-Jean, Cap Ferrat, is the darkest blue and has a terracotta pot with an orange tree at each corner.
3. Countess Munster's pool at Bampton shows a reflection of the lovely church spire.
4. Lord Esher, the architect, designed a swimming pool as a moat on three sides of his folly tower in Watlington Park with great success.

3

4

Shape

☐ Box and yew are very much quicker growing than many people give them credit for, especially if well fed and well watered. All over the world, I have seen people's attempts to control and modify the shape of their plants — shaped fruit trees, evergreens, lime and beech. Shaping plants implies using them in a design-conscious way, and the gardens that I find most attractive are those where shapes play an important part whether it is a line of cut trees or topiary.

1. Clipped cypress in the South of France making sublime abstract geometric shapes against the blue sky.
2. At Penshurst in Kent a window in a shaped yew hedge looks down into a Kent apple orchard untypical because of the way the apple trees are shaped.

☐ One of the greatest examples of a 'shape' garden is
Beckley Park, at present threatened by a motorway
within yards of its Tudor moat. Apart from two climbing
roses clinging to ancient apple trees, there is no colour
in this garden other than every kind of green, which has
'Castle pudding' yews thirty feet high, yards and yards
of box hedges, hornbeam garden temples, grass, mossy
brick paths, and a small cutting garden hidden away
behind yet more box hedging. It was all planted in 1924.
This style of green architecture has an overwhelming
interest for me, from the smallest clipped topiary shape
— perhaps in a modest-sized container — to the most
famous topiary garden in England at Levens Hall in
Cumbria. The variety of shapes, both geometric and

1/2. John Fowler created this small garden full of
shapes, and box-edged beds containing understated
flowers. A Portuguese laurel, one of a pair, stands in
front of one of the two great lines of clipped hornbeam
against a background of ancient trees on the fringe of
Dogmersfield Park.
3. In this garden near Orleans, two delightful clipped
shapes guard the turret staircase of an early house,
warmly clad with a rose.
4. At West Green House, Mr Alistair McAlpine has
revived an old topiary garden with great skill.
5. Part of the elaborate green garden at Beckley Park
which is ingenious and quite unique. This small garden
is not open to the public.

2

abstract, is almost limitless. These variations fascinate me, whether they are single animal shapes or vast sculptural blocks, extensions of the house, or boundaries or divisions between one part of the garden and another. Shapes can be formed into green buildings in their own right, and provide partial shelter in the midst of a summer storm. To achieve a proper shape for your green architecture often requires a concealed wooden or metal framework, as a certain amount of tying-in and support is needed. You must be decisive when you are working on such a project, and do remember the scale that you eventually want to arrive at. Feeding, weeding, watering and cutting are vital to good shaping.

6

7

8

10

6. Four of these sentinels guide the eye from this house in France to the garden.
7. The unique topiary garden at Haseley Court which at the time of writing is on the market, and one can only hope that a really sympathetic buyer will acquire it.
8. Some of the many inventive shapes at Beckley.
9. With perspicacity, the large stone plant containers on the private terrace at Chatsworth are no longer filled with bedding-out plants but planted with box and yew.
10. At Grimsthorpe Castle in Lincolnshire, the Earl of Ancaster's vegetable and fruit garden has splendid domes of the small-leaved box.

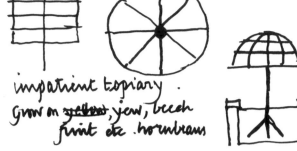

impatient topiary .
Grow on ~~yellow~~ yew, beech
fruit etc . hornbeam

Rosemary
how

Evergreen
honeysuckles + roses : montana   try [sketch] window
mind
for size .

1. The great yew rondel at Sissinghurst was planted in 1932. It forms the heart of the Nicolsons' famous garden. It is a wonderfully contemplative area in which to rest the eye between the delights of the other parts of the garden beyond.

2. The Duke and Duchess of Devonshire have made their own contributions to the great garden they inherited. They planted the Serpentine Walk, many other architectural beech hedges, the great lines of pleached lime as well as uncovering Paxton's monumental rock garden of boulders.

2

1. A simple corner of Powis Castle, where architectural yew borders stone and gravel paths; in the front, a splendid bank of hosta.

2. The Lutyens garden seat, by now almost excessively well known, designed by him for Lady Sackville for her garden in Brighton after lunch on the day that he received the commission for the Cenotaph, and here seen at Sissinghurst.

3. In the Duchesse de Brissac's garden near Paris, the topiary not only conceals the swimming pool, but is one of the finest examples of French topiary that I know: pom-poms, curves, buttresses, arches, ramparts — it adds very greatly to the house.

4/5/6. At Hidcote, Laurence Johnston created one of the great masterpieces of garden design in England since 1900. Working with an existing cedar of Lebanon as a basic feature, he shaped the holly in this photograph, and planted a yew hedge between the holly and the cedar; and formed (5/6) what is known as the Stilt Garden, to my mind, one of the most sublime pieces of green architecture in the world: austere, without colour, relying solely on its structure, its contrasts of texture between grass, gravel, hornbeams, and hedges with distant trees. It has had, and will always have, a profound influence on me.

1. These phallic shapes rising out of square bases make an important contribution to the garden design at Hidcote.

1

2. The extraordinary yew ramparts at Powis Castle, so ancient and so solid that the gardeners, when clipping them, can walk about on top.
3. At Great Dixter in Sussex, Christopher Lloyd has enchanting topiary in his vegetable and fruit garden.

4. At La Gaude, near Aix-en-Provence, the Baron de Vitrolle has made this dramatic labyrinth of box on an island encompassed by water in front of his château.
5. A corner of the topiary garden at Beckley, which, although planted by his father was really shaped by Basil Feilding himself.

Shape

The Dowager Lady Camoys has formed an enchanting garden around this great majestic shape, known to the villagers of Stonor as 'Queen Mary'. Her favourite rose, and one of mine, is Papa Meilland.

☐ Garden ornaments provide emphasis and accent in a garden, drawing the eye in a particular direction. Most ornaments, because they are solid and static objects such as urns, seats, columns or statues, provide a contrast with the living things around them. Ornaments can range from the simplest object – I recently spied a small concrete rabbit in the garden at Chatsworth – to the finest and most elaborate classical or eighteenth-century statue on a contemporary base. They can be made of any substance, and although I have suggested that they are usually man-made, a natural object – a specimen tree (which is perhaps why they are known as ornamental trees) or a piece of topiary – can equally be a garden ornament. Seats and chairs have an ornamental quality as well as a purely functional one, and I have dealt with these in a separate chapter.

1/2. Life-size garden statues used in dissimilar ways. The female figure in an opening in a dense hedge is dramatic against the light on the landscape behind her. The male figure is in a romantic, wild setting.

1

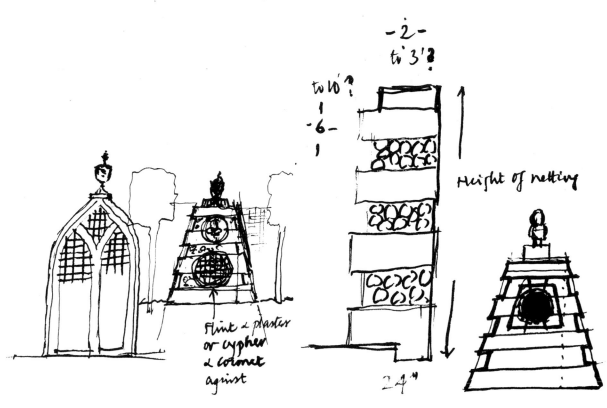

-2-
to 3'?

to 10'?
1
-6-
1

Height of netting

24"

Flint & plaster
or cypher
& coronet
aginst

1. This fine late eighteenth-century urn and pedestal have become partially engulfed by a manicured yew hedge at Hidcote.
2. A lovely eighteenth-century urn in stone rising out of a mass of roses.
3. At Sutton Park, Mrs Reginald Sheffield has created an entirely successful garden. Her husband acquired a pair of these early nineteenth-century stone vases, and

☐ There is a great deal of false snobbery attached to garden ornaments, the feeling that if they are not fine original works of some antiquity, then they are not worth having. It is not a snobbery I can share. I am a snob about plants and some sorts of planting, but I have a great respect for other people's sense of style in gardens. Ornaments are easy to improvise, or to make. I once made a most successful object from an old lightning conductor base which I discovered in a builder's yard. Many old foundries and scrap dealers contain items which, seen with a designing eye, could be used most effectively as garden ornaments. If your tastes lie more in the direction of urns and vases, then there are a number of manufacturers who make excellent reconstituted stone ones at reasonable prices, while some of the terracotta pieces are still more reasonably priced. There are numerous garden ornaments you can make yourself: open-work slatted pyramids for growing roses; concrete obelisks and columns. On the walls of my garden are two finials of five spires, made of nothing more elaborate than marine

placed them dramatically, and symmetrically, on the terrace.

4. Mr George Howard recently planted a large and handsome rose garden, to designs by Jim Russell, in memory of his wife, Lady Cecilia Howard. This handsome pair of eighteenth-century fluted urns make fine accents, particularly with their background of clipped hedges.

3

4

plywood coated with fibreglass and painted: they are very successful. In garden ornament, audacity is the key to success: use what you like in the way you like it.

☐ Garden gnomes are much sneered at, but I have seen them used most successfully, massed like a small army: and Candida Lycett Green has shown us how effective very ordinary objects and topiary can be in very small gardens. My tastes run on more classical lines, and I am lucky to have two quite good statues and some urns, but the essence of the successful use of garden ornaments is not so much the objects themselves, but the way in which they are used to create a sense of style and atmosphere. There is a great temptation to overload a garden with ornaments. This goes directly against their proper function as accents. I always consider very carefully how many, if even more than one ornament, a certain area of a garden can take.

☐ Each ornament should be placed with consideration; even the simplest pair of tubs with plants in them should be placed with thought on either side of a doorway, or a French window, or at the corners of a terrace. There is a glut at present of modern and ill-considered garden ornaments, often rather over-decorated and ostentatious — or with fake rustic finishes. There is a cement tub with what I can only describe as vertical crazy-paving and many hideous plastic containers which I would avoid at all costs. But most of the better manufacturers do one or two items which are well conceived. Look through as many catalogues as you can, and if possible see the items in position: many manufacturers have agents widely spread throughout this country and abroad. Always be careful about the colour and texture as well as the location; remember that they weather quite quickly in exposed positions. Ornaments perform much the same function as a jewel on a beautiful woman: they are the accents, the punctuation marks, and they should highlight and flatter.

☐ As well as free-standing objects, there are numerous embellishments which can be added to existing structures — acorns, balls, pineapples, obelisks, lion's

1

heads, and balustrades. Used in a limited and disciplined way they can add style. While these are available in reconstituted stone, there is no good life-size figure on the market at present, although there must be a demand for figures.

1. At Renishaw, in Derbyshire, Sir George Sitwell created a superb garden, and collected some fine Italian statuary for it. The fountain was recently added to his grandfather's circular basin by Mr Reresby Sitwell.

2/3. Fine eighteenth-century animal groups flank the private parterre at Chatsworth.
4. Plaster copy of the cast-iron dogs at St George's, Hanover Square, labradors originally cast in 1840.
5. An Italian Renaissance model, cast in Coadestone in the early nineteenth century, now at Swyncombe House.

Garden ornaments

☐ I like terracotta pots, although sadly the large twenty-inch diameter flower pots are now very hard to find in England. Some potters are prepared to make such things and there are also a number of commercial terracotta vases and pots on the market, some simulating baskets, which, with a couple of years of English weathering, are attractive.

☐ Remember with garden ornaments that scale is of prime importance. Too small a tub or pair of pots will look wrong because they are in too demanding a position. They could be successful in a smaller or less important area. The correct scale of an ornament or container is relative to the position in which it is used.

1. A fine cast iron statue flanked by a bower of roses at Sutton Park.
2. At Belvoir Castle, the Duke of Rutland's ancestor placed six fine figures by Caius Cibber, who was sculptor to King Charles II, in pairs descending a dell.
3/4. Alistair McAlpine commissioned Quinlan Terry to design this column for the end of an avenue at West Green House, Built in stone, it must be the finest garden ornament of our age.
5. A good white marble figure of a satyr in Kew Gardens.
6. One of the *termes* (a human face coming out of an architectural base), partially lost in a beech hedge in a delightful way, at Chatsworth.

3

4

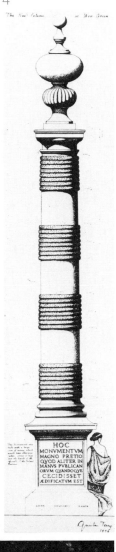

5

6

☐ Garden furniture is essential and particularly useful from a visual point of view. But it must be used with discretion. Too many chairs, benches or stools can look wrong. Permanent furniture like stone benches or seats must be clearly and thoughtfully positioned; there are delightful moveable garden seats with wheels. Dining chairs and tables for summer garden living will need to be stored during the winter.

1. A delightful wheelbarrow seat at a house in Yorkshire.
2. Delicate Regency Gothic garden chairs in wrought iron in the National Trust's most jewel-like garden, The Hunting Lodge at Odiham.
3. A typical Regency iron seat of great elegance.

4. A simple wooden garden seat under an ancient ivy-clad oak.
5. At Cranborne Manor atmospheric Edwardian folding garden chairs.
6. John Stephanidis designed these stylish garden chairs for his Dorset house.

1. Roderick Cameron's dining terrace in Provence has a stone-topped table and simple Provencal wooden rush-seated chairs.
2. Charmingly basic stools, chairs and table in an olive bower in the Biot home of M. and Mme Vulliod.
3. Stone-topped dining table with wicker stools on a Provençal terrace.
4. With Christian Badin of David Hicks France, I designed the dining room terrace furniture of the Schlumberger's Côte d'Azur house.

2

4

1. Lead peacocks and a pair of urns flank a charming garden seat of *circa* 1910.
2. A delightful segmented seat surrounding the base of an old tree.
3. A Victorian metal and wooden garden seat placed in a straight alcove in a new wall.
4. A solid wooden seat at Sissinghurst, the base of which is clad with creeper.
5. In the walled garden at Castle Howard, delightfully simple wooden seats in green alcoves.
6. At Floors Castle, the Duke of Roxburghe has this delightful example of Edwardian furniture in natural wood.

159

1. Mrs Lees-Milne set this iron seat on a small stone terrace and flanked it with symmetrical planting.
2. A handsome Chinese Chippendale garden seat in the Somersets' garden.
3. A charming variation on the wooden garden seat with slight Gothick influence.
4. At Syon House the Duke of Northumberland has the most practical Chinese Chippendale piece of garden furniture, the seats of which lift up so that after rain they may be let down and are dry.
5. A romantic cast-iron Victorian garden seat at Beckley Park painted dark green in the all-green garden.
6. A stylish white-painted piece of garden furniture.
7. A charming variation on Chinese Chippendale originally at Ditchley Park.
8. A garden seat made by David Verey in the spring garden at Belvoir Castle, which the Duchess of Rutland has recently restored.
9. A wheelbarrow seat at Haseley.

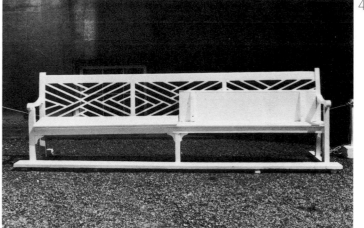

☐ I grow probably fifty per cent of my plants for possible use indoors.

☐ Constance Spry tells us to grow *Viburnum carlesii* in a pot and force it gently, so that it will scent a whole room. It should then be rested for two years out of doors. A number of things like gypsophila I grow because it is very attractive when in bloom, but when cut and dried it is an invaluable room-filler during the winter months. I like to have more than one or two dried bunches so that I can ring the changes during the winter months. It is not difficult to store them if you have a small shed out of doors. I grow a number of things for the house in pots, not only in a greenhouse, but also in the open air. Some of the roses which I dislike planted in a rose garden, or in a border, have merit when planted individually in pots and taken into the house to stand on the floor or on a side table. When my rhubarb begins to go to seed, I like to cut it when it looks very primeval and before it bursts. People often guess for some time as to what exotic flower this is. Herbs when they are burgeoning, at that awkward moment between the beginning of May and the middle of June when there are not too many flowers around, can be delicious when arranged as either one variety alone in a vase or as a mixed collection. I grow my hydrangeas, apart from white ones, for their extremely decorative use when dried for the winter, as well as for fresh arrangements in September.

☐ I have been through a remorselessly disciplined phase in my attitude towards gardens, and a few years ago I did not really want to see any flower near the house at all – I only wanted to see trees, gravel, lawn and water. At that time, I had a large walled garden which was entirely planted for cutting for the house, because even in that excess of austerity in my visual thinking I still relished vast bunches of flowers indoors. Now, in middle age, I am beginning to like flowers to come closer to the house; but perhaps that is because I now live in a less classical house. I am also becoming more catholic in my liking of different varieties and specimens. There is one vermilion Polyantha rose that I have disliked intensely for many years – it was one my parents were very enthusiastic about in the 1930s. But when I saw a line of them recently, it brought on such a pang of nostalgia that I shall now plant one or two, probably in pots or in my cutting garden. It is, after all, an intensely exciting and useful colour in July.

The Baronne Geoffroi de Waldener has built a superb conservatory on to her house in Provence, and these gothic glazed doors lead into it from her living room.

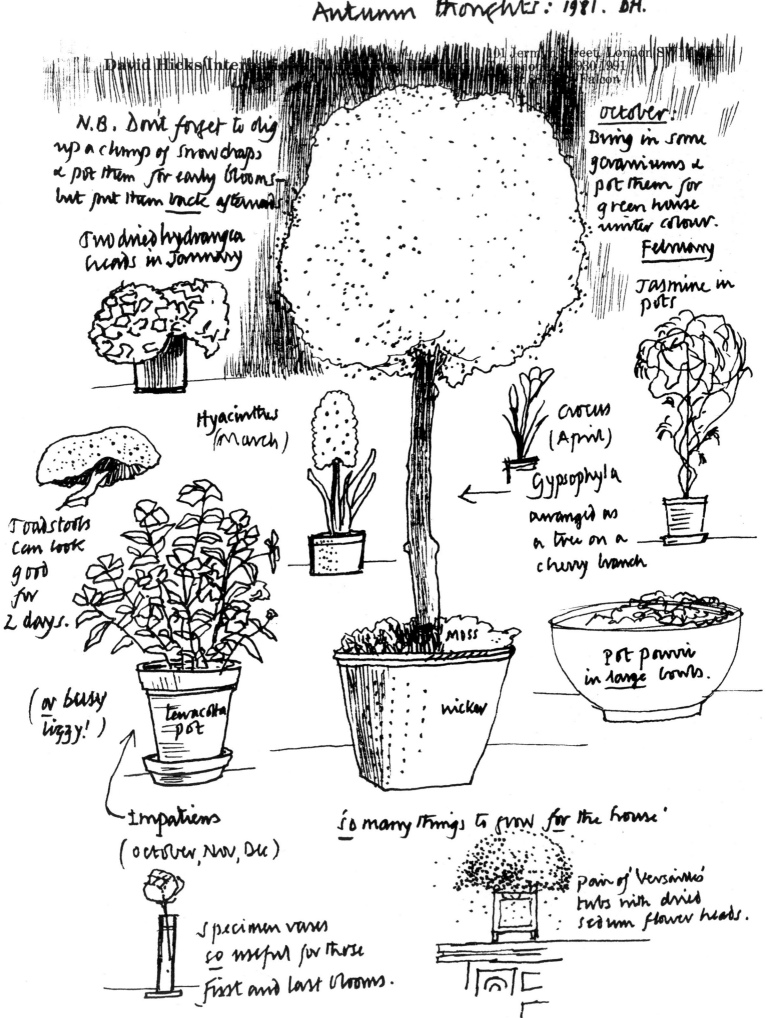

Autumn thoughts: 1981. DH.

David Hicks International ... 101 Jermyn Street, London SW1 ... Telephone 01 930 1991 ... Falcon

N.B. Don't forget to dig up a clump of snowdrops & pot them for early blooms — but put them back afterwards.

Two dried hydrangea heads in January

october! Bring in some geraniums & pot them for green house winter colour.

February Jasmine in pots

Hyacinthus (March)

crocus (April)

Gypsophyla arranged as a tree on a cherry branch

Toadstools can look good for 2 days.

(or busy Lizzy!)

terracotta pot

moss

wicker

Pot pourri in large bowls.

Impatiens (october, Nov, Dec)

So many things to grow for the house!

Specimen vases so useful for those first and last blooms.

pair of Versailles tubs with dried sedum flower heads.

1. A huge bunch of gypsophila, cut just as the white blooms were going over, which I placed in this vase ready for the following winter.

2. Winnafreda, Countess of Portarlington, grew wonderful plants for her house. Fifteen years ago I photographed this azalea in a Korean vase of perfect proportions in her house, Earlywood.

3. Kochia growing in a large earthenware pot, ready for indoor use.

4. I grow lilies in containers in my greenhouse, in order to bring them into the house.

☐ The conflict between informal and formal styles of gardening, which raged particularly strongly in the eighteenth and early nineteenth centuries, continues to this day. My approach to gardening with straight lines rather than cultivated 'informality' is very personal. But it gives me great pleasure to see herbaceous borders, if they are good ones, and to see informal gardens. It is perhaps because so much of my working life has been spent with houses and interiors that I tend to pay particular attention to the way gardens relate to houses. Buildings tend to be based on straight lines — or at least be fairly regular in their geometry, so I have a decided preference for straight lines near the house, contrasting with the informality of a partly man-made landscape beyond. What I really dislike are serpentine or free-form island beds anywhere. They are totally artificial; though

1

their owners suppose them to be very natural looking. Of course, you may have a house with a natural fall of land which produces curves and irregularities, and any attempt to cultivate or alter these natural shapes is bound to look contrived, unless the changes, such as forming terraces on different levels, are made with skill.

1/2. The contrast of style is shown, on the left with the tight, geometric approach, and on the right, a romantic traditional solution. Both are in Dorset, and complement totally different styles of building: to the left, Mr John Stephanidis', to the right, the Marchioness of Salisbury's' approach.

2

1. Lord De L'Isle's garden at Penshurst Place is in the process of development, which will add greatly to public enjoyment of it as the plan unfolds: apple trees separated from old roses by a yew hedge.
2/3. In two very different gardens, one in France and one in England, great style is achieved through year-round evergreen planting and strong linear design.
4. Two short architectural lines of trees give character to a garden.

3

4

☐ I grew up with parents who loved herbaceous borders, as did all their friends; and I suppose that I quite liked them too. But over the years, I have become less and less interested in them — and in fact actually despise certain people's herbaceous borders. It was not Nancy Mitford's description of the Kroesig's garden that made me detest herbaceous borders, but I read it with enormous relish, because she reiterated exactly my own view on most herbaceous borders. I think those which I most dislike are those which rely on delphiniums of a mid-blue, next to a raucous vermilion herbaceous poppy, with an unripe Burgundy-coloured rose growing on a wall behind it, pink valerian, a group of Polyantha roses, and a large patch of forget-me-not next to some orange marigolds. To this mixture could be added scarlet *Lychnis chalcedonica*, variegated lupins in mauve and pink — *ugh!* — faded cerise mallows, all massed together like a smudged water-colour. On the other hand there are herbaceous borders — which involve a lot of work and are somewhat dull out of season — that are very *subtle*. These have great clumps of *Crambe maritima* — at the back, large groups of white lilies, thalictrum, a burgeoning tripod of Constance Spry, or Ville de Bruxelles, a huge mass of grey-leaved hosta, a handsome group of pale pink poppies, gypsophila, a good carpet of bergenia, a contained bush of philadelphus, and all the other subtle ingredients of the good herbaceous borders that can be seen in those few great small gardens of England.

☐ The commonest fault that most people make with herbaceous borders is that their clumps are too small, and the variety of flowers and textures, leaves and plants, is ill considered. Bedding-out plants, to my mind, play a vital role in the subtle and successful herbaceous border.

☐ The longer one lives the more discriminating one becomes about plants and gardens and one's own likes and dislikes. I remember some years ago I positively disliked Bonsai trees. Now, I find them fascinating and acceptable, though I am not sure that I have yet found the way in which I want to use them. They are expensive to experiment with, but I feel that I shall possess one or two within the next decade.

☐ I detest rhododendron country, perhaps because I was at school in it, but in fact like certain varieties of the plant. In my small greenhouse I have Princess Alice and Fragrantissimum growing in pots, for although scraggy they are the best scented rhododendrons. There are ten in all. The others can grow out of doors, and, living in Oxfordshire, I grow these in tubs, in lime-free soil, and water them with rainwater. In this way I am able to have the varieties I like, although they are growing in an area which would not otherwise be suitable for them and they are controlled and contained. One is green-flowered and another green and pink which should be exciting.

☐ Red salvias I dislike even in Victorian bedding-out, but I have long had an ambition to plant a red garden, long before I saw the one at Hidcote, and salvias, planted in square blocks of colour, would certainly be part of this garden designed for August. I loathe hybrid tea roses in rose gardens, because for most of the year their habit of growth is so very ugly. These I think should be planted in straight lines in a cutting garden, for the house. However, having stated the rule, I immediately break it, for I also use hybrid tea roses discreetly to point up the colour of old roses in a bed. However, under these conditions the stunted form of the hybrid tea is masked by other plants, until it produces the wonderful colours for which I prize it.

☐ Delphiniums, in my view, have no place growing in a garden, a view with which I know many will disagree; I like them growing individually in pots, so that they can be brought indoors and stood on the floor. I got this idea from the Delphinium Society's stand at the Chelsea Flower Show in 1981.

☐ The majority of people in England grow giant sunflowers close to a wall and tie them to the house. I think they make small houses look ridiculous, and they certainly have no place against the wall of a great house so I like to grow them in large Versailles tubs, or in pots so that I can bring them into the house. I also like to grow them in a wild area and cut them in late September and early October and make a huge arrangement of them in a bucket on the floor.

☐ I really like: Acanthus, Alchemilla, Anchusa, Bergenia, Campanula, Dianthus, Digitalis, Euphorbia, Gypsophila, Helleborus, Hemerocallis, Hollyhocks, Hosta, Paeonies, Rodgersia and Roses.

☐ I really dislike: Asters, Aubrietia, almost all Chrysanthemums, Dahlias, especially the pom pom varieties, Dutch Iris, Gladioli, Lupins, Montbretia, *Muscari schizostylis*, Phlox, Pyrethrum, miniature roses and Blue Moon, Statice and Valerian, and in hot climates, my real aversion is for the dreaded Bougainvillea.

□ Building a garden for a new house on a new site, rather than a new house built within an old garden, poses very special problems. Firstly, the builder will probably have been extremely careless when bulldozing the site about removing the topsoil, and you will probably have to re-establish a layer of this. But do not stint on it: it will pay handsomely to have several loads of good-quality weed-free topsoil imported.

□ When starting from scratch, be sure to get your levels right. They are probably no longer natural levels, nor are they truly man-made; they are probably just the way the bulldozer driver left them. If you can afford it, it will save a vast amount of back-breaking work to employ a JCB to get the worst of the earth moving done.

Supervising the terracing of a new garden in an old setting. Huge machines like this, if well driven, can perform meticulously detailed operations, and save hours of manual labour.

□ Prepare your garden design on graph paper, so that you can scale it, peg it out with string and wooden pegs actually on the ground itself, and live with this for two or three days before committing yourself to decisions about what is going to be grass, gravel, shrubbery, roses or hedges. Look at it from the house, from all floors, from the end of the garden and from the sides. Look at your neighbours' gardens; see what plants do well on the local soil. Make friends with the local nurseryman, and find out what plants will be the most suitable. If you can persuade him to come and visit you, so much the better: after all, you may become a good customer. This is the stage at which to be totally determined. You must concentrate on certain kinds of plants and get to know all about them: buy books on them, read it all up, and start to feed your ground ready for the plants that you are going to use. If you live in a lime-rich area, definitely not rhododendron country, do not attempt to grow them. If you are *determined* to grow them, other than in tubs as I do, then you have a massive earth-moving task ahead of you. Even having done that, remember not to water them with anything other than pure, lime-free rain water.

1. Pleached lime trees, even when quite young, can provide an instantaneous effect.
2. The delightful apple orchard at Erddig, though very young, already has great style.
3. A short laurel tunnel in mid-development.
4. At Castle Howard, a fine pair of eighteenth-century urns are being enclosed by green arbours.
5. At Grimsthorpe Castle, cultivated American blackberries which are partially evergreen, and extremely decorative, used in an arched walk.
6. At Shute House in Dorset, wisterias have almost completed a circuit on arched supports.

1. My own hornbeams in Oxfordshire, which will be pleached, eight months after being planted. Hornbeam hedges behind the trees were planted in early December 1980.

2. The apple trees, a crenellated box hedge and yews, in early stages of development during the reconstruction of the garden at Erddig.

☐ I always like to see all new shrubs and trees in the earth before Christmas. Lawns are ideally sown in the third week of August, because, at this time of the year, rain or no rain, dew every morning is guaranteed; this does not occur in the spring. All new plants need constant attention against drying out, and being blown by wind. Be very careful in a new garden in using weedkiller; remember how easily it can be carried by the breeze on to vulnerable new plants. There is nothing to beat hand weeding or hoeing if you have the energy. There is an old saying, 'A year's seeding makes seven years' weeding', and it is, as I know to my cost, only too true.

1

☐ Personally, I do not grow vegetables, and I become increasingly irritated by the number of people who look at my garden, which is not small, and say 'And *where* are your vegetables?' It must be evident that unless you are a millionaire, you cannot, even with some professional help, have good lawns, well-kept trees, hedges, and a number of weed-free beds, and grow rows and rows of vegetables. So, the first, largely emotional, decision you have to make is the extent to which you intend to garden for things to eat. It is vital to decide, when planning a garden, whether it is going to be a vegetable garden, a flower garden, an architectural garden, or a mixture.

2

☐ I find when planting roses that the most important thing is to make sure that the ground is well loosened in and around the position where I am planting them, and then to firm them in really hard. There is nothing a rose dislikes more than being shaken by the endless winds of February and March. Whenever I go round the garden, and see something that might not be firmed in quite enough, I go in to the bed and make sure that it really is.

☐ Do not be too ambitious when buying and ordering plants. It is easy enough in the winter months, reading the glowing descriptions in the catalogues to think 'that will be marvellous here, that will be great there'; but remember that when it comes to the crunch period of the long, hot summer, and watering has to be done — and endless weeding confronts you — and the whole garden demands attention at the same time — some expensive though delightful things may in fact be wasted. Plant and design for what you think you can really cope with at the outset, bearing in mind that in later years you may want to cut back or reduce the garden. You can always add to what you have already, once you have had a couple of years seeing how it works out. It is pointless to have a garden which means that you are so busy working in it that you never have time to sit and enjoy it.

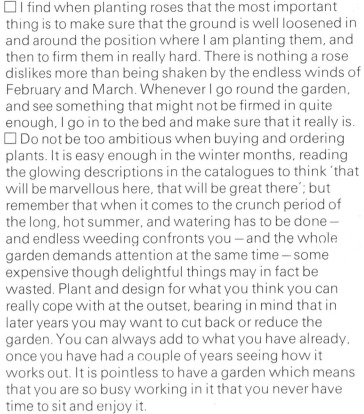

1. A fine example of *Catalpa bignonioides* at Kew. A most rewarding tree, and quick to grow in the right situation.

2. Standard rose trees have a particular rapport with Victorian cottages.

3. A sophisticated wooden pyramid in the Old Rose garden at Castle Howard, a good looking feature which is very telling in a new garden.

4. In a corner of Hampton Court, I noticed this delightful combination of standard fuchsias and low growing plants enclosed by box edging.

5. A pleached *allée* of hornbeam, planted in 1965 at Kew Palace.

6. Looking the other way down the hornbeam *allée* before it was cut in the early summer.

7. Straight lines of vegetables give an immediate and dramatic effect in a new garden. It is not *what* you grow or plant, but *how* you do it.

☐ An enormous problem which faces anybody planning a garden is how far they actually want to commit themselves to maintenance and upkeep in future. After all, those who do a garden, say in their thirties, have got a long life expectancy but somebody, like myself, who is making a garden at the age of fifty has got much less time, and therefore, one has got to plan the thing from the point of view of increasing old age and lack of help. It has to be planned in such a way that it can be cut back, in future years, into a manageable size. Romantic profusion, which has a great deal to contribute in garden design, can be allowed to go too far.

☐ When planning a garden — or any part of a garden — try to envisage what it will look like if it is left partially untended. Like a good general, plan a line of retreat. Some plants, as they become more abundant, can create a new and desirable effect. Trees as they grow larger become more dominant influences and they can be used to supersede other more time-consuming forms of planting. It is entirely possible to develop a garden from one which requires a great deal of time, worry and attention to one where, as the years advance, it is refined down to its few central elements, which can be maintained in their proper state with a much reduced expenditure of effort and money.

☐ Often, from the ground, a garden seems completely regular, symmetric and formal, but from the air or on a drawing it is not. In planning my new garden I sometimes found myself becoming over-preoccupied with straight lines and having everything at right angles; in dealing with old walls, I found that almost none of these were true. Allow the element of human error to creep in to the most formal of approaches. This gives a certain warmth to what could otherwise be too austere.

☐ In the planning stage you must determine what is going to be used for what. If you have a young family, you will need an area where they can make a mess — where they can have playpens, slides, and their toys. Many people now think in terms of a swimming pool, even in very small gardens, so it is worth considering where you would put one, even if you are not going to have one straight away. Think also where things like the filtration plant and the heating unit would go; where will you keep the pool cleaning equipment. Are you going at some stage to want a tennis court? If so, it is a good idea to put up the netting now, and plant it with honeysuckle, so that at the time when you actually want to have the tennis court constructed, you already have it hidden — after all, they are very ugly and it then will no longer obtrude in your garden. If you are going to think ahead in this way, remember that contractors for pools and tennis courts arrive with large equipment — so do not build a wall or plant the area without provision for their access.

☐ Croquet is popular with all ages, so part of your lawn may need to be sufficiently flat and large for this. Even in an existing garden you may find that the soil is not good all the way through, and it may be more economical in the long term to import some new topsoil rather than attempt to re-invigorate the poor existing soil.

☐ The placing of garden seats and ornaments is very crucial and before I build a brick base for a container or an urn, I lay the bricks out dry and place the object on the base in order to see if three or four weeks later I am really satisfied that I have got the height right, and the dimensions of the base correct.

☐ I have an Edwardian 'ladies' fork which my mother and her father before her used in five different gardens. I treasure this little fork. It is ideal for rooting out young docks in the middle of a concentrated planting where any larger tool would make too much mess. I also have a favourite old trowel, for planting out my bedding plants. But I have tried to equip my garden with as many aids as seemed prudent. Much of the hedge clipping can be done by machinery, though it is often necessary to hand-cut an old hedge before it is ready to be cut mechanically. Certainly the best watering device I have found is a sprinkler, operated by water pressure, which very slowly retraces the line of the hosepipe, so that you can leave it alone for three hours and it will water a set path through the garden while you get on with other things.

☐ For pleached trees, and any of the more architectural types of clipping, you will need to devise some special means of reaching high up on to the sides and tops of trees that would otherwise be unreachable. For our last garden, we devised a tall stand which allows you to reach the tops of box-cut chestnut trees twenty feet from the ground. There are now various demountable towers available for house painting, often on hire, which are excellent. It is always worth seeking out a hire shop — the Yellow Pages of the telephone directory list them — for they often stock many of the larger items you may need only once or twice a year, but which will make the construction or maintenance of your garden very much easier.

☐ For mowing on steep banks we use an air cushion rotary mower, and for areas where grass meets walls a strimmer. Be careful not to let the cutting wire get too close to the base of any climber, but if you do damage one, paint the cut immediately with Arbrex. For the lawns we use a cylinder motor mower, and delight in the striped band effect which is most people's idea of a successful lawn. With a new lawn it is often a good idea to leave the grass box off so that the cuttings provide a mulch for the new growth. For our 'beard-length' grass, which separates the lawn from the long grass in the early summer, and then when the long grass is cut to beard length for the rest of the summer, we use a power scythe.

☐ When new trees arrive for planting, there is frequently some minor damage. Always cut off vertically any damaged twigs with secateurs, and paint the cut over. When an old tree has a branch broken off by storms, it should always be cut vertically, so that the water does not rest on it, and painted with Arbrex to seal the wound.

1. The positioning of an important garden ornament such as this needs very careful consideration. Because it was too grand in design for the house, I specifically planted hornbeam trees which will be followed by hedges so that they will engulf the urn when looking back at the house; but when looking out from the house, it will be completely visible. The final effect will of course take many years to achieve.

2. At Castle Howard, a gutsy Vanbrugh entrance arch.

Simple pyramids such as these could be copied for far less grand situations, and using readily available materials, at relatively little cost.
3. I designed this variation on a Versailles tub for my own house, and, in this photograph, I am firming in a giant sunflower.

In 1978, when we knew that we were going to move from Britwell to The Grove, I immediately started to plan the new house and the new garden within the old walls and farm buildings. Apart from the dreaded elm disease, The Grove lives up to its name and we are fortunate to have some fine old trees, among them a specially good Ilex.

1/2/3. Do not let contractors work when you are away: be there and work with them. They prefer it and you will get infinitely better results.
4. I pierced an existing wall and formed a gothic archway. I bought a door for £2.00, which when transformed became the starting point of my home-made greenhouse.
5. A year later, an openwork gothic garden door, set off by two iron bollards, partially screens the view of the dark green painted greenhouse.

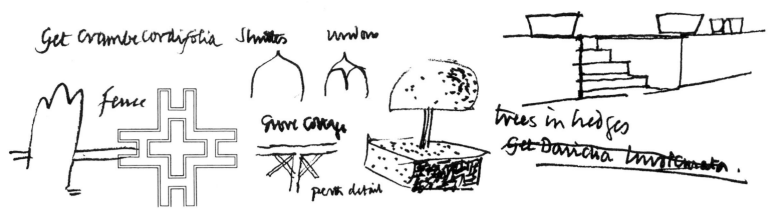

□ In the south garden there were a pair of evergreens of considerable age, but though planted equidistant from the drawing room, they were not matching in shape or height for one was a yew and the other a cypress. In the end we decided to have them down and embark on a strong architectural planting of pleached hornbeams with hedges behind. In the west garden two large and useful barns dominated the prospect while the country was flat and uninteresting, so I decided to plant a clipped double line of horse chestnuts with a modest avenue of the same tree beyond, cut an opening in the hedge in the middle distance and a vista in the copse at the far end of the prospect. All this distracts the eye from the previously over-dominant barns. To the east, farmland scattered with ancient oaks makes an excellent contrast, and on the north side I have two lines of pollarded limes hiding a tennis court built in a three-sided walled garden.

□ We took over a garden which had been neglected by various tenants who had planted the ugliest of roses — now all replaced — so it was exciting to start from scratch, first with plants I moved from our old garden, choisyas, hellebores, bergenia, *Iris stylosa*, hydrangeas, old roses, honeysuckles and acanthus — many of which I potted — and then, with those wonderful catalogues from rose growers and plantsmen, started ordering. I even visited garden centres, though they are a poor substitute for the nurseries of my youth, with 'Mr So and So' personally taking one round and giving endless useful information while taking the order with a stubby pencil.

□ Mr Madgen who moved from Britwell with us began to get the one existing lawn into condition, and in late August 1980 he sowed the present splendid lawns, before tackling in November and December the mammoth tree-planting exercise. With someone who is really enthusiastic to help, a great deal can be achieved, and we shall always be grateful to him and to Stephen Strange.

1. In the old walled garden, I planted two rows of lime trees leading to the tennis court.

2. At the top of this double line of limes I erected two plastered breezeblock piers and surmounted them with dogs. Later, to left and right of the gate piers, a beech hedge will mask the tennis court entirely. Breeze is of course infinitely cheaper than brick or stone and, well finished, just as effective.

2

3/4. Having constructed my swimming pool, I then levelled the earth around it to a predetermined level. One year later the lawn is established but not by any means perfect. The chestnuts in place, though not able to be cut for at least five years, one of a pair of urns, and the stable building on the left pierced with a gothic doorway. The planting is already beginning to take on the terrace.

4

☐ A neglected garden is a paradise for weeds — their names are only too achingly familiar — but I tend to have a relaxed attitude to them after late July. This attitude relates only to the weeds in my rose garden and my simple borders, not to the squares around the new trees, which are not only mulched with bark but are constantly weeded. I would really prefer a profusion of annuals to weeds but there is so little time to get everything perfect, and I actually think late summer weeds add a little romance.

☐ The garden design I have embarked upon is one I really like; it just needs a little time and well-fed exuberant planting in between the strong lines of design. I spend hours contemplating what I've done and what I will do to embroider it, but in the main I am pleased with what I set out to achieve. I have certainly planted for the end of my life, but I am content to wait and see it mature. Each year will bring more stature and volume to the planting, and I have designed it in such a way that I can cut it down in size and reduce the responsibility for maintenance — or my son can. The strong central architectural lines must always be kept trim, but the minor flower planting could be abandoned if non labour-intensive gardening had to be countenanced. It was great fun planting it, it is a lasting chore maintaining it, but I love to watch it develop.

1

2

4

5

3

1/2. The south side of the house needed a sunblind to control the light and to add atmosphere to an undistinguished façade. Below this I designed a simple Chinese Chippendale seat, which looks well with the window.

3. One side of my line of about-to-be-pleached hornbeam, with a fine eighteenth-century stone urn, the position of which I considered very carefully, as they are very expensive to move on account of their weight.

4. Another heavy but charmingly carved stone urn, inconsequentially placed against a background of old trees.

5. An openwork gothic door identical to the one that leads to the greenhouse, overwhelmed by a giant sunflower in a large dark green painted tub, which will eventually hold a twelve-foot sculptured beech tree.

6. A simple brick mounting block, which I surmounted with a cast concrete slab with a Soanesque detail.

6

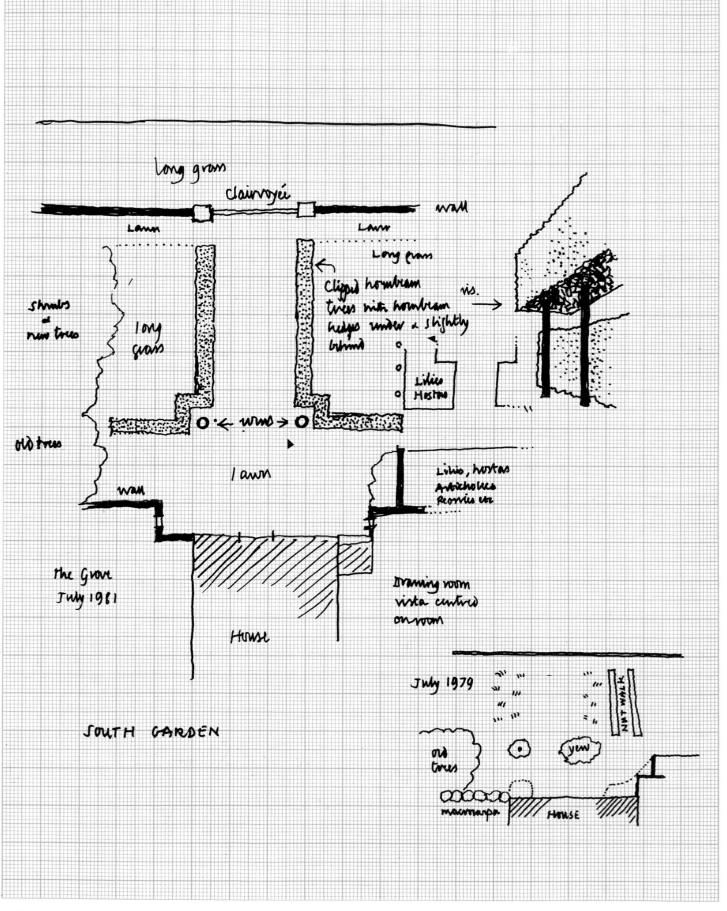

long grass

clairvoyée

wall

Lawn

Lawn

Long grass

Clipped hornbeam
trees with hornbeam
hedges under a slightly
raised

vis.

shrubs
of
new trees

long
grass

Lilies
Hostas

old trees

wall

← wind →

lawn

Lilies, hostas
artichokes
Peonies etc

the Grove
July 1981

Drawing room
vista centred
on room

House

July 1979

SOUTH GARDEN

old
trees

yew

NUT WALK

macrocarpa   HOUSE

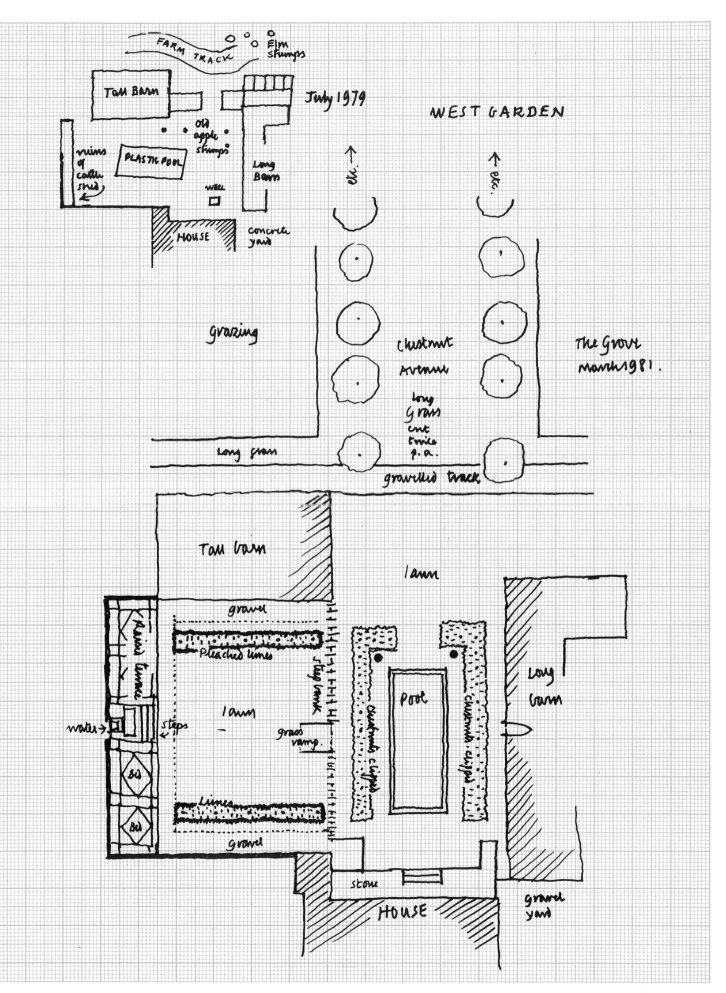

FARM TRACK

Elm stumps

Tall Barn

July 1979

WEST GARDEN

old apple stumps

ruins of cattle shed

PLASTIC POOL

Long Barn

etc. →

etc. →

WELL

HOUSE

concrete yard

grazing

chestnut avenue

long grass cut twice p.a.

The Grove march 1981.

long grass

gravelled track

Tall barn

lawn

gravel

Pleached limes

step bank

chestnut chapel

chestnut chapel

Pool

Long Barn

water →

steps

lawn

grass ramp

Bd

Bd

Limes

gravel

stone

HOUSE

gravel yard

Suppliers

Nurseries, etc. Abercorn Plants
Barons Court, Newtownstewart, Co. Tyrone, N. Ireland

Allwood Bros
Clayton Nurseries, Hassocks, Sussex

Avon Bulbs
Bathford, Bath, Avon

Peter Beales (Roses) Ltd
Intwood Nurseries, Swardeston, Norwich

Walter Blom & Son Ltd
Coombelands Nurseries, Leavesden, Watford,
Hertfordshire

William Crowder and Son Ltd
Horncastle, Lincolnshire

Exbury Gardens Ltd
Exbury, Southampton, Hampshire

Fibrex Nurseries Ltd
Harvey Road, Evesham, Worcestershire

Fisks Clematis Nurseries
Westleton, Saxmundham, Suffolk

Hillier Nurseries Ltd
Ampfield House, Ampfield, Romsey, Hampshire

Kelways Nurseries, Langport, Somerset

John Mattock Ltd
Nuneham Courtenay, Oxfordshire

Notcutts Nurseries Ltd
Woodbridge, Suffolk

Southdown Nurseries
Southgate Street, Redruth, Cornwall

Toad Hall
Henley on Thames, Oxfordshire

Thompson and Morgan Ltd
London Road, Ipswich, Suffolk

Waterperry Horticultural Centre, Wheatley, Oxfordshire

Garden ornaments	Chilstone Sprivers Estate, Horsmonden, Kent
	Haddonstone Ltd The Forge House, Church Lane, East Haddon, Northamptonshire
	Minsterstone Ltd Station Road, Ilminster, Somerset
	Pradeli, Poterie Provençale, Biot, Alpes Maritimes
	Stone Art Ltd Haylands, Kimblewick Road, Great Kimble, Buckinghamshire
Garden Furniture	The Chatsworth Estate Office, Carpenters' Shop Edensor, Derbyshire
	Rex Knott Ltd Boston Road, Horncastle, Lincolnshire
Underfoot	Leake's Masonry, Louth, Lincolnshire
	Jas Strutton and Son Ltd 283 Kingsland Road, London E2

Many houses open to the public have garden centres,
and at Chatsworth there are plans to manufacture some
of the garden seats illustrated in this book.

Plants I like

□ Few things are more daunting than the vast list of flowers which accompanies most books about gardening. This list is of plants I like and use *at the moment.* My taste changes, and many plants figure in this list which would not have done so a few years ago. There are other plants named in the text but this list comprises most of those which I would choose for planting a garden from the beginning, along the lines I have set out in this book.

Acanthus spinosus
Aconites
Alchemilla mollis
Allium giganteum
Buddleias (all of them)
Choisya ternata
Clematis Nellie Moser
C. Marie Boiselot
C. Perle d'Azur: this flowers in August
C. Lasurstern
Cornus mas
Crambe cordifolia
Crocus chrysanthus Ladykiller
C. Kathleen Parlow
C. Pickwick
C. sativus (autumn-flowering)
Daphnes (all of them)
Eremurus bungei
Erigeron
Euphorbias:
E. griffithii Fireglow
E. polychroma
E. robbiae
E. wulfenii
Fritillaria imperialis: yellow or orange

F. meleagris
Gunnera manicata
Gypsophila
Hellebores (all of them)
Hemerocallis
Hostas (all of them)
Hydrangea Madame E. Moullière
H. libella
Iris germanica The Citadel
I. Lady River
I. sibirica
I. stylosa
Jasmines (all of them)
Lilacs (all of them)
Lilies (all of them)
Lily of the Valley
Magnolia:
M. grandiflora
M. mollicomata
M. sargentiana robusta
Mignonette (*Reseda odorata*)
Nicotiana Evening Fragrance (from Suttons)
N. affinis Daylight (from Thompson and Morgan)
Paeonies: all of them including tree paeonies
Philadelphus: all of them

Polygonum baldschuanicum
Rhododendrons (scented)
R. Countess of Haddington
R. Crayssum
R. Formosum (gibsonii)
R. Fragrantissimum (excellent in a glasshouse)
R. Johnstoneanum
R. Lady Alice Fitzwilliam
R. Lindleyi (has white, carmine and green flowers)
R. Michael's Pride (has a most attractive lime-green flower).
R. Polyandrum
R. Princess Alice (tender)
Rosa Albertine
R. American Pillar
R. banksiae
R. Constance Spry
R. Duc de Guiche
R. Fantin Latour
R. Félicité et Perpétue
R. gallica officinalis
R. Gloire de Dijon
R. Grüss an Aachen
R. Karlsruhe
R. Lady Hillingdon

R. Lady Seton
R. Lady Waterlow
R. La Reine Victoria
R. Louise Odier
R. Mme Alfred Carrière
R. Mme Caroline Testout
R. Mme Isaac Pereire
R. Mme Pierre Oger
R. Papa Meilland
R. Paul Neyron
R. Peace
R. Sir Cedric Morris
R. Souvenir de la Malmaison
R. Super Star
R. Swan Lake
R. Variegata de Bologna
R. Viridiflora (the green rose)
Sedums (all of them)
Snowdrops (Galanthus spp.)
Sparmannia africana
Thalictrum dipterocarpum Hewitt's Double
Tulip Apricot Parrot
T. Plaisir
T. Queen of Bartigons
Viburnums (all of them)
Vitis coignetiae

Books to read

A few essential reference works will feature on any gardeners' list; I have included only those books which I have found the most stimulating.

The Education of a Gardener
Russell Page (Collins, 1971).
The Country Gardener
Penelope Hobhouse (Phaidon, 1976).
Variations on a Garden
Robin Lane-Fox (Macmillan 1974).
The Englishwoman's Garden
Alvilde Lees-Milne and Rosemary Verey
(Chatto & Windus, 1980).
Plants for Connoisseurs
Peter Coats (Collins, 1974).
A Gardener's Diary
Joan Law-Smith (National Trust of Australia 1976).
Garden Notebook
Constance Spry (Dent, 1940).
The English Flower Garden
W Robinson (John Murray, 1944).

It is worth bearing in mind that any public library can obtain almost any book, in or out of print.

Credits

The National Trust
Barratt (Developments) Ltd
Guildford Bell
Peter Burton
Greg Fitness
Jon Harris
Geoff Hunter
Mallaby's Photographic Workshop
Jean Louis Menriesson
David Mlinaric
Nicholas Primrose-Jenkins
Olive Smith
Fleur Vulliod
Wimpcy Ltd

Throughout this book, the author has worked with a
twenty-year-old Rolleiflex, which can still be serviced
and repaired by Wallace Heaton of New Bond Street,
London.